CHILD WELFARE PROBLEMS

Prevention, Early Identification, and Intervention

Greta L. Singer
Marcia G. Rachlin
Maybeth C. Cassidy

UNIVERSITY
PRESS OF
AMERICA

Copyright © 1983 by

University Press of America, Inc.™

P.O. Box 19101, Washington, D.C. 20036

All rights reserved

Printed in the United States of America

ISBN (Perfect): 0-8191-2875-9
ISBN   (Cloth): 0-8191-2874-0

ACKNOWLEDGEMENTS

This project was supported by Grant #02CT00011080, awarded by the Department of Health and Human Services.

We wish to express our gratitude to the Grant-In-Aid Committee of Monmouth College, West Long Branch, New Jersey for the grant that helped to make this book possible.

TABLE OF CONTENTS

PREFACE

This text is designed to provide a total learning experience in the field of Child Welfare. The materials incorporate sociological, psychological and cultural concepts to create a course offering which establishes a link between academic knowledge and professional practice. The material is designed for a bachelors or masters social work curriculum, in-service staff training, and continuing education programs.

Each chapter of the text includes five distinct components which enable the instructor or trainer to present a comprehensive learning experience:

1. Didactic material
2. Questions for study and discussion
3. Experiential exercises
4. References
5. Audio visual materials

The chapter begins with didactic material which focuses on theoretical concepts and current trends in the field of Child Welfare. Challenging questions for study and discussion are included to encourage further exploration of the subject matter. Two experiential exercises have been designed to supplement the text. Each exercise has as its goal the synthesizing of cognitive theory with practical application. To facilitate further research, each chapter offers selected references. The chapter concludes with a selected listing of related audio visual materials which can be used to augment the teaching/training design.

Chapter One begins by defining child welfare, placing child welfare services in a historical perspective and highlighting the relevant points in current child welfare legislation.

Chapter Two defines systems theory and uses the concepts to provide a framework for understanding the family. The changing American family is then discussed.

Chapter Three examines the sources of stress that can lead to family breakdown. The impact of racism and class bias is included here.

Chapters Four, Five and Six cover child neglect

child abuse and sexual abuse. Characteristics of the parent and child "victims" are discussed here. Each chapter includes a section on prevention, early identification and intervention.

A separate chapter has been devoted to each of the supportive, supplementary and substitute services. Chapter Seven covers supportive services. Parents Anonymous, as a major child welfare self-help group, is described. Chapter Eight defines the supplementary services, including Income Maintenance, Homemaker Services, Day Care Programs and Protective Services. Chapter Nine describes the growing movement toward home based care services.

The concluding chapters of the text focus on foster care and adoption. Chapter Ten examines the foster care system. Chapter Eleven highlights the major issues in adoption.

The exercises have been designed to provide a pleasant, educationally valuable learning experience. It is ultimately the responsibility of each instructor to ensure that this intent is maintained through the responsible facilitation of each activity.

Each exercise should be carefully introduced to ensure the students' understanding of the purpose and procedure. In those exercises which require the disclosure of personal experiences or feelings, the pass option should be explained. Those participants who do not choose to respond to any personal question are free to say, "I pass." A pass answer is always acceptable.

This text presents an overview of the child welfare field. Special problem areas such as deliquency, handicapped children, and institutional services have been excluded in the belief that such subjects require more detailed examination.

The education and training of competent professionals in the field of child welfare offers a unique challenge to the educator. This text addresses this challenge by presenting a comprehensive educational experience which blends cognitive theory with personal reflection and self-assessment.

CHAPTER I

INTRODUCTION TO CHILD WELFARE

The well-being of the family and the rearing of healthy, well-adjusted children is one of this nation's highest priorities. In our everchanging, highly mobile society, where approximately one out of three marriages ends in divorce and the extended family has all but disappeared, this goal is an increasingly difficult one to attain.

The field of child welfare is concerned with the well-being of children. The child welfare goal is to promote the optimal development of the child's bio-psycho-social potential in harmony with the values and needs of the community.

People are entitled to develop their own unique potential. The best chance for optimum growth and happiness is usually within the child's own family. Parents have the right to rear their children in accordance with their own beliefs and values without outside interference. These ideas form the basis of United States social policy. However, when the quality of care the child receives falls below the minimum acceptable level, society must intervene to ensure the well-being of the child. Finding the balance between parental rights and responsibilities and those of society remains as a difficult child welfare issue.

The parent, the child, and society form a constantly interacting triad. Child Welfare Services are based on the knowledge that, at times, the well-being of the child may be endangered because of a conflict or inadequacy in any one part of the triad.[1]

Rights and Responsibilities of the Parent

The parent is expected to meet the basic physical needs of the child, including food, clothing, shelter, health care, as well as the emotional needs including love, security, protection, guidance and supervision. The parent has the responsibility for socializing the child by teaching the behavior that is seen as accept-

---

[1]Lela Costin, Child Welfare Policies and Practices, New York: McGraw Hill, 1979, p. 4.

1

able in our society, and by serving as a role model.

The parent determines the child's present and future existence. The likelihood that the child will get the care needed is dependent on the psychological capacity and social adjustment of the parent.

Rights and Responsibilities of the Child

The child has rights to care, protection, and guidance from the family. In turn, the child has an implicit responsibility to respond with age-appropriate growth and development.

In 1930, at the White House Conference on Children, a children's charter was developed enumerating the needs and rights of the child. (See Table I, p. 7). In 1951, the United Nations developed an international Declaration of Rights of the Child (See Table II, p. 10).

Rights and Responsibilities of Society

Society serves the regulatory power. Society's interest and values are represented through the application and development of broad standards which apply to all in relation to children. Through the courts and social agencies, society must act on the child's behalf when the care falls below the minimum acceptable level. Society has the responsibility for assessing its own inadequacies, and then, for legislating for the development of needed child welfare services.

Circumstances Requiring Child Welfare Services

Most children live with their families as a reasonably well-functioning system. Child welfare services are required when the parents or children are unable or unwilling to fulfill their respective responsibilities. Examples of this are situations where the following occur:

A.	Role Unoccupied	E.	Interrole Conflict
B.	Role Incapacity	F.	Child Incapacity
C.	Role Rejection	G.	Deficiency in Community Resources[2]
D.	Intrarole Conflict		

[2]Alfred Kadushin, Child Welfare Services, New York: Macmillan Publishing Co., Inc. 1980 pp. 13-23.

A.   Role unoccupied may refer to a temporary condition as in parental hospitalization or a permanent situation as parental death.

B.   Role incapacity exists when the parent is unable to meet responsibilities due to illness, a handicap, or parent skill deficiency.

C.   Role rejection is evidenced by the parent neglecting or even abandoning the child.

D.   In a two-parent family, there are times when the parents have problems between them with respect to defining and handling their respective parental roles. If they are unable to resolve their intrarole conflict, certain aspects of the child's care may be neglected or inappropriately handled.

E.   At times, other obligations may interfere with the implementation of the parent role causing an inter-role conflict. A job or the demands of extended family members take parents away from their parental responsibilities.

F.   A child's incapacity or handicap may make excessive demands on the family, preventing the parent from adequately caring for the handicapped child or other children in the family.

G.   A deficiency of community resources or lack of access to them may prevent parents from adequately implementing their role. The lack of job opportunities, adequate housing, or health services will make it difficult for the parent to care for the child.

Each of these circumstances, resulting from a parent incapacity, the special needs of a child, or limitations within the community calls for intervention by society through child welfare services.

Types of Child Welfare Services

Child welfare services have been broken down into three different categories:

1.   Supportive Services
2.   Supplementary Services
3.   Substitute Services

Supportive Services are designed to strengthen the ability of the parents to meet their children's needs. The family remains intact, with the parent in control. These services are primarily found in the form of voluntary counseling services. Supplementary Services are designed to supplement inadequacies in parental care. Income Maintenance, Homemaker Services and Day Care represent the supplementary child welfare services. Substitute Services are designed to substitute for parental care, temporarily or permanently. These are in the form of foster care, group homes, institutions or adoption.

Historical Trends and Principles of Child Welfare

In our early history, when individuals were unable to care for themselves, they became the responsibility of the locality. A child needing care was auctioned off to the lowest bidder. A family agreed to care for the child for a predetermined, regular sum of money or goods. The lowest bidder gained ownership of the child. An older, able-bodied child was indentured. The child was trained and cared for in exchange for labor.

Gradually, a more humanitarian philosophy developed. With the realization that children had special needs different from those of adults came state involvement through specialized state institutions such as orphanages, reform schools, institutions for the blind, deaf and mentally retarded. At this point, the emphasis was on removing children from their homes and treating them in isolation from their families. No attempt was made to help the family. Poor children were most frequently removed from their families.

In 1870, the first reported case of child abuse came to the attention of the authorities. Mary Ellen was being severely abused by her foster parents. Church workers tried to have her removed from her home. She finally did receive help through the SPCA on the basis that she was a member of the animal kingdom. This case prompted the development of the Society for the Prevention of Cruelty to Children in 1875.

In the late nineteenth and early twentieth century, a national interest in children was growing. Much of the early child mistreatment was by foster and adoptive parents and within institutions. Once the sanctions for societal child abuse were removed through the abolition

4

of child labor, incarceration, and chain gangs, the focus of attention moved within the family structure. In this period came the establishment of child labor laws, the juvenile court, and the passage of mother's pension laws.

In 1909, under the leadership of Theodore Roosevelt, the first White House Conference on Children convened. Subsequent conferences have been held at ten-year intervals since that time. The establishment of the United States Children's Bureau to investigate and report matters pertaining to child welfare was an outgrowth of this conference.

Since 1935, child welfare programs have been administered under the Social Security Act of 1935. The philosophy of maintaining the family as a unit has grown throughout the twentieth century. Passage of the Social Security Act of 1935 represents the most significant federal effort to provide for the needs of families and their children. The Act has greatly extended the responsibility of government for services and programs in support of the family. The following amendments are examples of legislation which continue to broaden child welfare services.

Title IVA - Title IVA, passed in 1967, encouraged states to develop daycare services for children of welfare recipients. The government reimbursed the state expenditures on a 75:25 matching basis.

Title IVB - Title IVB authorized grant-in-aid and matching funds to states for establishing or expanding services for the protection of neglected and abused children. These services were not to be limited to those eligible for financial assistance.

Title XX - Title XX, passed in 1975, provided block grants to states for the development of social services. Half of these services were required to go to those receiving benefits under Aid to Families with Dependent Children (AFDC) and Supplemental Security Income (SSI). The state had the authority to decide what programs should be funded.

The Social Security Act provides the funding source for the programs in support of the family. Other legislation which has passed has specified new standards which must be met in order to receive these funds.

Child Abuse Prevention and Treatment Act of 1974

This legislation holds a non-punitive philosophy, providing protection for the child rather than punishment of the parent. A child is a person with rights. Something can be done about the mistreatment of children and all people have the responsibility for protecting the child.

The first part of the Act, the reporting law, requires professionals to report suspicion of child mistreatment to authorities for investigation. It is a punishable crime to withhold information. The Act encourages individual citizens to report and provides immunity from civil suit to anyone who reports in good faith. The second part of the legislation provides for the development of central registries to receive, store, and disseminate information about child abuse and neglect. The central registries are the subject of much controversy. Such registries provide information not otherwise available, but they have been abused and misused. Some critics argue that too many people have access to central registry information, thereby threatening confidentiality. Unsupported claims may mistakenly remain in the register.

This Act provides assistance to states for the development of child abuse and neglect programs and supports research in these areas. It further established the National Center for Child Abuse and Neglect within the Children's Bureau, which acts as a clearinghouse for information on existing child protection programs. The Center also supports research and the development of new programs in the area of child welfare. This legislation sparked much interest in child mistreatment as is evidenced by the numerous programs and publications that have come into existence since its passage.

The Adoption Assistance and Child Welfare Act of 1980

This legislation, adopted in November 1980, emphasizes preventive and home-based child welfare services. Through research came the awareness that large numbers of children were remaining in foster care for long periods of time. This legislation sought to prevent the unnecessary separation of children from their families. In order to receive maximum federal financing,

6

all efforts to prevent placement must be made prior to removing the child from the home. Once a child is placed in foster care, the case must be reviewed every six months. The family must continue to receive services aimed at returning the child to the home. Permanency through reunification with parents is the ultimate goal of this legislation. When reunification is not possible, the termination of parents' rights and adoption are emphasized. Funding for permanent placement is also provided through this legislation.

TABLE I*

THE CHILDREN'S CHARTER

President Hoover's White House Conference on
Child Health and Protection, recognizing
the rights of the child as the first
rights of citizenship, pledges
itself to these aims for
the Children of America

I. For every child spiritual and moral training to help him to stand firm under the pressure of life.

II. For every child understanding and the guarding of his personality as his most precious right.

III. For every child a home and that love and security which a home provides; and for that child who must receive foster care, the nearest substitute for his own home.

IV. For every child full preparation for his birth, his mother receiving prenatal, natal, and postnatal care; and the establishment of such protective measures as will make child-bearing safer.

V. For every child health protection from birth through adolescence, including: periodical health examinations and, where needed, care of specialists and hospital treatment; regular dental examinations and care of the teeth; protective and preventive measures against communicable diseases; the insuring of pure food, pure milk, and pure water.

VI. For every child from birth through adolescence, promotion of health, including health instruction and a health program, wholesome physical and mental recreation, with teachers and leaders adequately trained.

VII. For every child a dwelling place safe, sanitary, and wholesome, with reasonable provisions for privacy, free from conditions which tend to thwart his development; and a home environment harmonious and enriching.

VIII. For every child a school which is safe from hazards, sanitary, properly equipped, lighted, and ventilated. For younger children nursery schools and kindergartens to supplement home care.

IX. For every child a community which recognizes and plans for his needs, protects him against physical dangers, moral hazards, and disease; provides him with safe and wholesome places for play and recreation; and makes provision for his cultural and social needs.

X. For every child an education which, through the discovery and development of his individual abilities, prepares him for life; and through training and vocational guidance prepares him for a living which will yield him the maximum of satisfaction.

XI. For every child such teaching and training as will prepare him for successful parenthood, homemaking, and the rights of citizenship; and, for parents, supplementary training to fit them to deal wisely with the problems of parenthood.

XII. For every child education for safety and protection against accidents to which modern conditions subject him--those to which he is directly exposed and those which, through loss or maiming of his parents, affect him indirectly.

XIII. For every child who is blind, deaf, crippled, or otherwise physically handicapped, and for the child who is mentally handicapped, such measures as will early discover and diagnose his handicap, provide care and treatment, and so train him that he may become an asset to society rather than a liability. Expenses of these services should be borne publicly where they cannot be privately met.

XIV. For every child who is in conflict with society the right to be dealt with intelligently as society's charge, not society's outcast; with the home, the school, the church, the court and the institution when needed, shaped to return him whenever possible to the normal stream of life.

XV. For every child the right to grow up in a family with an adequate standard of living and the security of a stable income as the surest safeguard against social handicaps.

XVI. For every child protection against labor that stunts growth, either physical or mental, that limits education, that deprives children of the right of comradeship, of play, and of joy.

XVII. For every rural child as satisfactory schooling and health services as for the city child, and an extension to rural families of social, recreational, and cultural facilities.

XVIII. To supplement the home and the school in the training of youth, and to return to them those interests of which modern life tends to cheat children, every stimulation and encouragement should be given to the extension and development of the voluntary youth organizations.

XIX. To make everywhere available these minimum protections of the health and welfare of children, there should be a district, county, or community organization for health, education, and welfare, with full-time officials, coordinating with a state-wide program which will be responsive to a nation-wide service of general information, statistics, and scientific research. This should include:

(a) Trained, full-time public health officials, with public health nurses, sanitary inspection, and laboratory workers.

(b) Available hospital beds.

(c) Full-time public welfare service for the relief, aid, and guidance of children in special need due to poverty, misfortune, or behavior difficulties, and for the protection of children from abuse, neglect, exploitation, or moral hazard.

For EVERY child these rights, regardless of race, or color, or situation, wherever he may live under the protection of the American flag.

* Table I - Copy Children's Charter - White House Conference, 1930

TABLE II*

DECLARATION OF THE RIGHTS OF THE CHILD

Principle 1 - The child shall enjoy all the rights set forth in this Declaration. All children, without any exception whatsoever, shall be entitled to these rights, without distinction or discrimination on account of race, color, sex, language, religion, political or other opinion, national or social origin, property, birth or other status, whether of himself or of his family.

Principle 2 - The child shall enjoy special protection and shall be given opportunities and facilities, by law and by other means, to enable him to develop physically, mentally, morally, spiritually and socially in a healthy and normal manner and in conditions of freedom and dignity. In the enactment of laws for this purpose the best interests of the child shall be the paramount consideration.

Principle 3 - The child shall be entitled from his birth to a name and a nationality.

Principle 4 - The child shall enjoy the benefits of social security. He shall be entitled to grow and develop in health; to this end special care and protection shall be provided both to him and to his mother, in-

cluding adequate prenatal and postnatal
care. The child shall have the right to
adequate nutrition, housing, recreation,
and medical services.

Principle 5 - The child who is physically, mentally,
or socially handicapped shall be given
the special treatment, education, and
care required by his particular condition.

Principle 6 - The child, for the full and harmonious
development of his personality, needs love
and understanding. He shall, whenever
possible, grow up in the care and under
the responsibility of his parents, and in
any case in an atmosphere of affection
and of moral and material security; a
child of tender years shall not, save in
exceptional circumstances, be separated
from his mother. Society and the public
authorities shall have the duty to extend
particular care to children without a
family and to those without adequate means
of support. Payment of state and other
assistance towards the maintenance of
children of large families is desirable.

Principle 7 - The child is entitled to receive education,
which shall be free and compulsory, at
least in the elementary stages. He shall
be given an education which will promote
his general culture, and enable him on a
basis of equal opportunity to develop his
abilities, his individual judgment, and
his sense of moral and social responsibility, and to become a useful member of
society. The best interests of the child
shall be the guiding principle of those
responsible for his education and guidance;
that responsibility lies in the first place
with his parents. The child shall have
full opportunity for play and recreation,
which should be directed to the same purposes as education; society and the public
authorities shall endeavor to promote the
enjoyment of this right.

Principle 8 - The child shall in all circumstances be
among the first to receive protection and

relief.

Principle 9 - The child shall be protected against all forms of neglect, cruelty and exploitation. He shall not be the subject of traffic, in any form. The child shall not be admitted to employment before an appropriate minimum age; he shall in no case be caused or permitted to engage in any occupation or employment which would prejudice his health or education, or interfere with his physical, mental or moral development.

Principle 10- The child shall be protected from practices which may foster racial, religious and any other form of discrimination. He shall be brought up in a spirit of understanding, tolerance, friendship among peoples, peace and universal brotherhood and in full consciousness that his energy and talents should be devoted to the service of his fellow men.

* Table II - Copy U. N. Declaration of Rights of the Child, 1951

FOR STUDY AND DISCUSSION

1. When the quality of care a child receives falls below the minimum acceptable level, society must intervene to ensure the child's well-being. Minimum acceptable level is a difficult standard to determine. Discuss the factors that must be considered in determining this minimum acceptable level.

2. The attitude toward and treatment of children has undergone much change throughout our history. Trace this history, highlighting the major philosophical and legislative changes.

3. The Child Abuse Prevention and Treatment Act of 1974 and the Adoption Assistance and Child Welfare Act of 1980 are two major pieces of child welfare legislation. Discuss their overall philosophy and major provisions.

Student Exercises

These exercises are designed to provide a non-threatening introduction to the experiential segment of the class. The activities focus on the student's personal values and experiences as they relate to family life. In each activity, students should be encouraged to become more conscious of the potential effect which familial beliefs and experiences may have on their performance as a child welfare worker.

EXERCISE #1   PERSONAL COAT OF ARMS

MATERIALS: One copy of the blank coat of arms for each student (see sample)

Pencil or pen

PROCEDURE:

1. The instructor should begin by explaining the activity to students. The introduction should include a brief discussion of the history of heraldry and the Coat of Arms.

   The family coat of arms was developed long before most people were literate. The coat of arms provided a personalized pictoral. representation of a family's heritage. The symbols on the coat were selected to represent the family's occupation, social status, strengths, and accomplishments. In some instances, the coat of arms also included a written family motto.

2. The instructor explains that each student will now create a personal family coat of arms. The coat should reflect each student's family of origin or current family system. (In those rare instances when the student cannot identify with any specific family, ask the student to answer the questions as projections of an ideal future family system).

3. Distribute copies of the blank coat of arms to each student.

4. Instruct students to answer each of the following questions by drawing a picture, design or symbol in the appropriate area of the sheet. Words may

13

only be used for Question #6. Students need not be
concerned about the caliber of their art work.

a. What one symbol best represents the personality
    or "flavor" of your family?

b. What do you see as one of your family's
    greatest accomplishments?

c. What is one special gift, tangible or intan-
    gible, which you have received from your
    family?

d. Which family member has had the most influence,
    positive or negative, on the life you lead
    today?

e. What stands out in your mind as one particu-
    larly pleasant family activity?

f. If you were to choose a motto for your family,
    what would it be?

PROCESSING:

1. Students should form triads.

2. Allow a few minutes for students to explain those
    areas on the coat of arms which seem to be most
    important to them.

3. Return to full group discussion. In this discus-
    sion, the instructor should encourage students to
    explore the potential influences which personal
    family values and experiences could have on their
    activities as practitioners.

    The discussion might include the following:

    a. What ways might your family experiences in-
        fluence your role as a practitioner?

    b. How can you become more conscious of personal
        family values?

    c. What have you learned from this activity?

FAMILY COAT OF ARMS

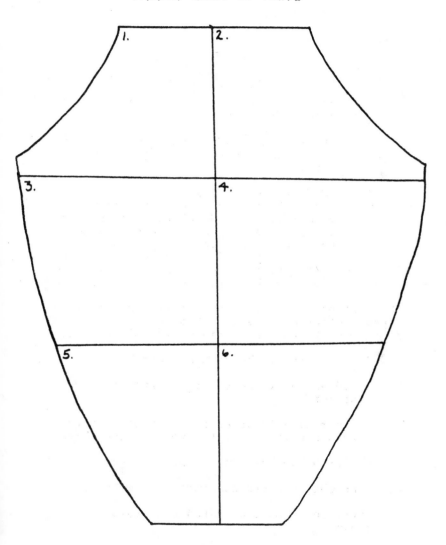

EXERCISE #2   FAMILY MESSAGES

MATERIALS: One copy of the "Family Message Sheet"
                  for each student (see sample)

                  Pencil or pen

PROCEDURE:

1.   The instructor should introduce the activity with
     a very brief discussion of family messages. Mes-
     sages, as they are used in this activity, refer to
     those rules, spoken or unspoken, which are part of
     a family's belief system.

2.   All students should stand in the middle of the
     room. The instructor gives specific directions
     for the exercise.

          I am going to read a list of familiar family
          messages. After each message has been read,
          please walk to one side of the room or the
          other, depending on your response to the
          message. If the message was part of the be-
          lief system of your family of origin, please
          walk to the right side of the room; if it was
          not, please walk to the left side of the room.

3.   The instructor should read the list of family mes-
     sages. After each message has been read, the stu-
     dents move to the appropriate side of the room.

     a.   Children should be seen and not heard.

     b.   Children should be sheltered from family
          conflict.

     c.   If sacrifice is necessary, parents should
          always sacrifice for the good of the child.

     d.   Children have as many rights as their parents.

     e.   Good children are successful in school.

     f.   Every child must be given good religious
          training.

     g.   Child rearing is the primary responsibility of
          the mother.

16

h. The father should have the last word in all family decisions.

i. Good children always obey their parents.

j. The success of a family is measured by the success of the children.

4. Ask students to return to their seats.

5. Distribute copies of the Family Message Sheet. Ask each student to respond to each message again. This time, students should respond by noting their personal belief at the present time. Students should note their responses by circling either AGREE, DISAGREE or UNDECIDED.

PROCESSING:

1. As the instructor reads out the list of messages in Step #3, it may be helpful to ask a few general questions to the group after they have responded by moving to the appropriate side of the room.

   Questions might include the following:

   a. Why did you go to this side of the room?

   b. How did your parents demonstrate this message?

   c. Was this message spoken or simply implied?

   d. Did most of your friends' families operate with the same messages?

   e. As a child, did you agree with this message?

2. In a large group summary discussion, the instructor should encourage students to reflect on their responses. Discussion questions might include the following topics:

   a. Which of your family messages do you agree with today?

   b. Which of your family messages do you disagree with today?

   c. Do you believe that there are definite right

17

and wrong responses to any of these items?

d. What are some additional family messages which could have been included on this list?

e. What influence could your family messages have on your activities as a practitioner?

FAMILY MESSAGE SHEET

DIRECTIONS: Please respond to each of the items below
by circling the response which corresponds
with your present personal beliefs:

1. Children should be seen and not heard.

    AGREE   UNDECIDED   DISAGREE

2. Children should be sheltered from family conflict.

    AGREE   UNDECIDED   DISAGREE

3. If sacrifice is necessary, parents should always
    sacrifice for the good of the child.

    AGREE   UNDECIDED   DISAGREE

4. Children have as many rights as their parents.

    AGREE   UNDECIDED   DISAGREE

5. Good children are successful in school.

    AGREE   UNDECIDED   DISAGREE

6. Every child must be given good religious training.

    AGREE   UNDECIDED   DISAGREE

7. Child rearing is the primary responsibility of the
    mother.

    AGREE   UNDECIDED   DISAGREE

8. The father should have the last word in all family
    decisions.

    AGREE   UNDECIDED   DISAGREE

9. Good children always obey their parents.

    AGREE   UNDECIDED   DISAGREE

10. The success of a family is measured by the success
    of the children.

    AGREE   UNDECIDED   DISAGREE

References

Brenner, R., Children and Youth in America, Boston: Howard University Press, 1970.

Child Welfare Strategy in the Coming Years, Washington: U.S. Department of HEW Office of Human Development, 1978.

Costin, L. B., Child Welfare: Policies and Practice, New York: McGraw Hill Book Company, 1979.

DeLone, R., Small Futures: Children, Inequality and the Limits of Liberal Reform, New York: Harcourt Brace Jovanovich, 1979.

Frederickson, H.; Mulligan, R.A., The Child and His Welfare, San Francisco: W.H. Freeman & Co., Inc., 1972.

Gross, R.B., The Children's Rights Movement: An Overcoming of the Oppression of Young People, New York: Anchor Books, 1977.

Hobbs, N., The Futures of Children, San Francisco: Jossey Bass Publisher, 1975.

Murphy, L., Growing Up in Garden Court, New York: CWLA, 1974.

Reid, J., Child Welfare Perspectives, New York: CWLA, 1979.

Scherr, A., Children and Decent People, New York: Aliven L. Schorr, 1974.

Senn, M.J., Speaking Out for America's Children, New Haven: Yale University Press, 1977.

Steiner, G., The Children's Cause, Washington: Brookings Institution, 1976.

Wight, R.R. ed., Our Troubled Children: Our Community's Challenge, Columbia University Press, 1966.

Zeitz, D., Child Welfare Services and Perspectives, Wiley, 1969.

CHAPTER II

SYSTEMS THEORY:
AN APPROACH TO UNDERSTANDING THE FAMILY

Systems theory as a conceptual model offers a way of thinking that emphasizes interaction and relatedness rather than individual characteristics. It examines an entity in relation to things it affects and is affected by. Since social work does emphasize the person in relationship to his environment, systems theory provides a relevant framework for the study of the family.

Systems Theory

A system is a whole composed of interrelated and interdependent parts. It has boundaries; something is or is not a part of the system. A system has a structure made up of those parts included in the system. A system must be viewed from a frame of reference. One individual or thing can be a part of many different systems. The whole being greater than the sum of its parts is an emergent quality which has an important effect on the whole as well as its parts. This interrelatedness gives rise to new and different qualities that are a function of the interrelatedness. A change in one part affects the system as a whole and leads to changes in its parts. Individuals or things may interact in subsystems within the system.

Systems Theory Approach to the Family

The family is a system. It is a special group of individuals greater and different from the sum of the individual members. The boundary and structure are defined by the members of the family. The family exists as an entity within a social context. Individuals are subsystems within families. The family carries out many of its functions through subsystems.

The Family

The traditional American family is the nuclear family. It is composed of two adults of different sexes living together within a sexual relationship, and their children. The family consists of three primary interrelated subsystems: the marital couple, the parent-child subsystem, and the sibling systems of relationships. The family is held together by numerous

21

mutually reinforcing functions. It provides the context in which the marital couple meets its sexual needs.
As the child rearing unit, the family has responsibility
for procreation, definition of clear boundaries between
generations, and for the transmission of culture, social
roles, coping skills and communication skills. This
responsibility is carried out by both teaching and role
modeling. The family must provide for the emergence of
the child from childhood, through adolescence to adult-
hood. Finally, the family, as the unit from which
society develops, provides for economic support and
division of labor among its members.

Developmental Tasks in a Two Parent System

At the beginning of the marriage, the couple must
develop a routine for living. This includes who will
do what household chores, who will work where, how they
will spend their money, what they will do with leisure
time, etc. The couple is setting up a series of transactions in which the way one spouse behaves, triggers
a reaction in the other. The repetition of these transactions provides the organization for the family. In
order for the new marriage to solidify, the spouses
must separate from their family of origin and develop a
new set of loyalties. The relationships with their own
parents, and siblings, and the new relationships with
in-laws change their role and place in the system. For
smooth functioning, each member of the couple must not
only make this break, but the family of origin must
accept and support it. Other relationships change as
well. Some individual friends become couple friends.
The nature of the relationship with individual friends
changes. Demands of the outside world such as one's
job and hobbies also affect the family. A comfortable,
mutually satisfying adjustment in each of these areas
provides a solid base in the development of the family
and the formation of a new system.

The birth of a child causes a radical change in
the family organization. Spouses become parents;
parents become grandparents; the child forms the base
for a sibling subsystem. Becoming parents requires much
physical and emotional time and energy. The care and
nuturance of a child can be a consuming, all encompassing, and at times, overwhelming experience. The
birth of each subsequent child further changes the
family system, its tasks, and its patterns of interaction.

The parenting tasks of the family with small children primarily involve care and nuturance. Socialization of the children remains primarily within the family. As the children grow older, peer interaction and extra-familial forces provide added dimensions to which the family must accommodate. In the family with adolescents, conflicting needs for autonomy and guidance provide for a new set of tasks. To survive, the family must meet the challenges of both internal and external change, while maintaining stability and continuity.

Problems

Problems in the family system often occur at times of transition or change. The severity of the problem for the family is significantly affected by the availability and effectiveness of individual strengths and external supports.

Reality is usually different from one's expectations. This can be a pleasant surprise, but it may also be a disappointment and the source of a problem. The feeling that, "he or she was so different before we got married" or "I thought that problem would resolve itself once we were married" may indicate the potential for problems. In the marital relationship, two different people are coming together. This "differentness" in itself is an opportunity for growth and enrichment. When the differences of one conflict with the expectations and needs of the other, problems may arise. The differences that initially attracted marital partners to each other may become sources of irritation. Vivaciousness becomes overwhelming and quietness becomes isolating. There is need for accommodation by both partners. If they are able to do so, the relationship will grow. If not, stress and conflict may arise. The ability to make these accommodations is based on each individual's emotional make-up and their existing support systems. In a functional relationship, one continues to think, act and feel as an individual, yet welcomes the contributions and "difference" of the other. In a dysfunctional relationship, an attitude such as "if you loved me, you'd want what I want" prevails.

The parental role is an emotionally gratifying one, yet it can also be experienced as a draining one. Therefore, it is filled with the opportunity for conflict and stress. People decide to become parents for a variety of reasons. A moral responsibility to perpetuate the human race underlies many of these reasons. Continuity and perpetuating one's own flesh and blood are also common reasons. Parenthood provides the opportunity to relive vicariously past experiences with the child, while helping the child to avoid one's own past mistakes. The child may represent the parent's hope for fulfilling something the parent did not accomplish. The child provides a new purpose for life, where two people can unite in an effort to influence the development of a new life.

Not all children are conceived under ideal circumstances. The child may be unplanned and the parents may not be economically or emotionally able to provide for this new family member. The couple may feel overwhelmed by the total responsibility that is being thrust upon them. A couple may decide to have a child to solve marital problems. They soon find that this would-be solution provides a host of new problems. The care of a new baby is so demanding and all encompassing that it may cause one or both parents to isolate themselves from previous relationships and activities. Although the parent may initially be willing to do this, isolation is at the root of many potential problems. The spouse may feel very threatened by and jealous of this child who is now getting all of the attention. A husband's feeling that his wife no longer has time for him is common. A mother-child subsystem is forming and the father may feel that he is an outsider.

The Changing American Family

In our constantly changing society, the family is being transformed accordingly. There are new roles, expectations, norms, and values. One must change and adapt behavior in accordance with societal changes in order to comfortably function within this environment. Very few things are concrete, explicit or lasting. This ambiguity and lack of stability can be stressful. With the weakening of the extended family, tradition and continuity are becoming more difficult to sustain. There are new expectations of the institution of marriage, as evidenced by the continually increasing divorce rate. For economic reasons as well as for reasons of self-fulfillment, women are combining their career and motherhood roles. This has caused new expectations for shared child rearing and household tasks. Assorted theorists, all with conflicting ideas, are providing us with new standards of child rearing. The ambiguity and conflicting ideas may only serve to raise the parent's anxiety level about proper child rearing practices.

New Traditional Roles

The traditional American family as defined earlier no longer prevails. New forms of family styles have developed in increasing numbers. One parent families are more common than ever before. Single parents are becoming parents by choice, not just by accident. Single parents are being approved as adoptive parents. Fathers as well as mothers are taking the responsibility for raising children alone. Shared parenting, where the child is a part-time member of two families, is growing in acceptance. Homosexual couples are able to live in the open and continue to raise their families. Each of these alternatives poses a new set of issues and requires further accommodation by society, its members and institutions.

FOR STUDY AND DISCUSSION

1. The tasks of the family with small children differ from those of the family with school-aged children. These differ further from the tasks of a family with adolescents. Discuss the different family and child rearing tasks at the different stages of development.

2. Apply the concepts of systems theory to the family.

3. For the family to survive in our constantly changing society, it must change as well. Discuss some of the changes the family has undergone in the last two decades, and the reasons behind these changes.

Student Exercises

These exercises focus on two key segments of the class content. The first exercise is designed to simulate the experience of adding a new member into a family system. In the second exercise, students have an opportunity to consider the plethora of developmental tasks which the parent or parents must undertake when a child is included in the family system.

EXERCISE #1   LET ME IN

MATERIALS: None

PROCEDURE:

1. The instructor begins by asking for four volunteers to participate in a role play. Assign numbers 1, 2, 3, 4 to each of the participants.

2. Ask role play participants #3 and #4 to leave the room temporarily while instructions are given to remaining role play participants and other class members.

3. Once #3 and #4 have left the room, the instructor asks #1 and #2 to sit facing each other in the front of the room and then explains the role play situation to them:

> You have been good friends for a long time. In the past few months, you have both become extremely busy with school and work, making it almost impossible to get together and share private conversation time. Today, you have some free time to chat. You happen to be discussing your future plans for school, jobs, or whatever. This is a special time for you. You really don't want any interruptions.

4. The instructor explains the observers role to the remaining students in the class:

> You will not take an active role in this situation. You are simply asked to observe the process of the interactions, watching for significant verbal and non-verbal responses which occur as the role play progresses.

26

5. The instructor should now leave the room to explain the roles to #3 and #4.

   You will be called back into the room one at a time. Your role is to join into the group with the other active participants.

6. The instructor should return to the classroom and ask #1 and #2 to begin the role play. Allow about three minutes for the conversation to become well established.

7. After approximately three minutes, the instructor should call in #3 with no further instructions or assistance. Allow about five minutes of inter-action among #1, #2, and #3.

8. The instructor should call in #4 with no further instructions. Again, allow about five minutes of interaction among the four members.

9. At an appropriate point, the instructor should terminate the role play.

PROCESSING:

1. Return the class focus to a full group discussion. Begin by asking role play participants to explain some of their feelings as they went through this activity. Be sure to encourage each role player to respond. Ask observers to share any observations which they may have made during the role play. Try to keep the focus of these comments on observations of role player responses. Avoid discussions in which role players or observers try to replay the scenario with different words.

2. Ask class members to relate this role play situation to a family system which is attempting to adjust to the inclusion of new family members. What observations can be made about this adjustment process as a result of experiencing the role play?

3. Some possible specific questions -

   a. Questions to #1 and/or #2:

      1) How did you feel when #3 appeared?

27

2) How did you feel when #4 appeared?

3) Were there any differences to your response to #3 and #4? Why?

4) What did #3 and #4 do which annoyed you?

5) What did #3 or #4 do which made you feel better about their inclusion?

6) What, if anything, could #3 or #4 have done to make you feel better about their inclusion?

7) What, if anything, could you have done to make them feel more comfortable?

b. Questions to #3 and #4:

1) How did you feel when you first came back into the room?

2) What thoughts went through your mind as you tried to gain entry into the group?

3) What verbal or nonverbal messages were you receiving from other members of the group?

4) Did you ever feel accepted by other group members?

5) What, if anything, could you have done to smooth out your entry process?

6) What, if anything, could #1 and #2 done to make you feel better?

7) If you could replay this scene, would you change any of your behaviors?

8) If you were a child and #1 and #2 were adults, would you want them for your parents?

c. Questions for observers:

1) What did you see happening as the scenario progressed?

28

2) Were there any significant nonverbal responses which you observed?

3) How did you feel as you watched the scenario develop?

4) In your opinion, which group members had the most difficult roles? Why?

5) Do you now wish that you had volunteered to participate?

EXERCISE #2   THE JOB OF THE PARENT

MATERIALS: Blank paper or newsprint, at least 8 to 12 sheets

Pencil or pen

PROCEDURE:

1. Instructor begins by dividing the class into four subgroups. Ask students to join with other members of their subgroup in a separate area of the room.

2. The instructor should explain the activity to all students:

In the next few minutes, we are going to work together to develop a list of developmental tasks which are part of the process of child rearing. To allow for more comprehensive lists, each group will focus on those tasks which apply to a specific age range.

3. Assign age ranges to each of the four groups:

Group #1 - birth through two years
Group #2 - three years through five years
Group #3 - six years through twelve years
Group #4 - thirteen years through seventeen years

4. Ask each group to select a recorder to compile the group's list. Supply the recorder with newsprint and magic markers and/or paper and pen.

5. Explain the specific task:

29

You will now have approximately five minutes
to generate a comprehensive list of the
parenting tasks which must be fulfilled for
children in your group's designated age range.
Many tasks may appear on more than one list.
Some items on your list may be general (i.e.
provide health care); some items may be quite
specific (i.e. teach tooth brushing). Be
resourceful and creative and have fun.

6. Allow approximately five minutes for groups to
    work. If suggestions are still being made by
    group members you may choose to extend the time.

7. Once groups have completed their preliminary lists,
    explain the second phase of the task:

    Now that you have generated your lists, please
    set some priorities. As a group, evaluate
    your lists and select the ten tasks which you
    see as most crucial to the rearing of well-
    adjusted children. Again, you will have
    approximately five minutes.

8. Once time has elapsed, return subgroups to full
    class focus and process the information.

PROCESSING:

1. Ask the recorder from each subgroup to share the
    results of the group's prioritized lists. If time
    permits, record these lists on newsprint or on a
    blackboard.

2. Use the information from these lists to generate
    class discussion. Questions might include the
    following:

    a. What new insights have you made as a result of
        participating in this activity?

    b. From the lists in front of you, what do you
        see as the most challenging tasks of child
        rearing?

    c. Why do so many families seem to have difficulty
        fulfilling these tasks?

    d. Do you think most couples are aware of these

responsibilities before they become parents?
What can be done to make them more aware?

e. Considering the scope and complexity of these
    tasks, what do you think should be done to
    assist parents in their roles?

References

Carter, B. & McGoldrick, M., Family Life Cycle, Gardner Press, 1980.

Egleson, J., Parents without Partners: A Guide for Divorced, Widowed or Separated Parents, Dutton, N.Y., 1961.

Greenberg, L., A Tiger by the Tail: Parenting in a Troubled Society, Chicago, Nelson Hall, 1974.

The Joys and Sorrows of Parenthood, Scribner, N.Y., Group for the Advancement of Psychiatry, Committee on Public Education, 1973.

Le Shan, E., How to Survive Parenthood, N.Y., Random House, 1965.

Minuchin, S., Families and Family Therapy, Cambridge, Massachusetts, Harvard University Press, 1974.

Satir, V., Conjoint Family Therapy, Palo Alto, CA., Science and Behavior Books, Inc., 1967.

Audio Visual Materials

Adapting to Parenthood, Audio Visual Services, The Pennsylvania State University, University Park, PA., 16802.

The Family: Lifestyles of the Future, Audio Visual Services, The Pennsylvania State University, University Park, PA., 16802

Love is for the Byrds, Audio Visual Services, The Pennsylvania State University, University Park, PA., 16802.

Mental Health and the Family, Human Relations Media, 175 Tompkins Ave., Pleasantville, N.Y., 10570

Our Changing Family Life, Audio Visual Services, The Pennsylvania State University, University Park, PA., 16802

Parents, Audio Visual Services, The Pennsylvania State University, University Park, PA., 16802

CHAPTER III

THE BREAKDOWN IN FAMILY FUNCTIONING

In 1979, the National Center of Child Abuse and Neglect estimated that 1.5 million children are maltreated by their parents each year. The scope of this problem has prompted interest in understanding who these people are and why this mistreatment is occurring. Such an understanding of this problem begins with an examination of the forces which operate within all family structures.

Relevant Forces Operating in Relation to the Family

    A. Individual capacities
    B. Cultural factors
    C. Specific life experiences
    D. Community institutions

    A. Individual capacities

        One's individual capacities, including one's physical and mental health, intelligence, personality characteristics, and past experiences as a child, are probably the most significant and constant in determining one's behavior.

    B. Cultural Factors

        The cultural factors, including values and attitudes toward children, violence, corporal punishment and religion, also contribute to an individual's behavior.

    C. Specific Life Experiences

        Specific life experiences contribute to the individual's ability to function well. Each person's coping ability is influenced by such factors as marital relationship, employment situation, housing condition, economic security, and support systems. The individual's relationship with community institutions may affect behavior as well.

D. Community Institutions

Community welfare organizations exist on three
levels. General community institutions such
as police, fire departments, and schools exist
for everyone's use. The problem oriented services such as mental health centers and anti-
poverty agencies are available for people with
specific types of problems. Those with problems related to child welfare may interact
with protective service agencies, child guidance clinics, family service agencies, the
juvenile and family court, schools, and health
service agencies.

These agencies exist to strengthen the family
support system. However, they may represent
new sources of stress for a troubled family.
When the experience with an agency is negative
as in an authoritarian or punitive contact, it
may exacerbate the situation, resulting in
family breakup or disintegration.

When the family's situation and relationship to
these relevant emerging forces is experienced as positive and supportive, it helps to strengthen family ties
and increase coping skills. A combination of negative
forces operating in conjunction with each other can lead
to the breakdown of the family. Family disintegration
can also result from economic hardship, health problems
or emotional illness. One form of breakdown exists in
the form of child maltreatment as in child neglect,
child abuse and sexual abuse.

Institutional Racism and Class Bias

Institutional racism and the resultant discrimination in all aspects of life contribute to the problem
of child mistreatment. In large urban centers where
the population is heavily poor and minority, the
schools continue to turn out children who cannot read.
The fact that after decades of effort we are still
unable to teach poor children to read suggests that it
is not a very high priority.[1] The illiteracy leads to
student dissatisfaction, as evidenced by the number of
poor students who get into trouble, the poor school

[1]Naomi Chase, A Child is Being Beaten, New York,
McGraw Hill, 1976, p. 35.

attendance, and the high dropout rate. The lack of education contributes to the high minority unemployment rate in the cities and all of the accompanying problems of poverty. Inadequate housing, and lack of economic security, negatively affect morale and decrease the tendency of a minority male to marry and remain to support his family, which in turn contributes to the high rate of single parent families among minority group members.[2]

For the single parent, family life is pressured and stressful. When one parent attempts to combine employment demands with child rearing responsibilities and personal need fulfillment, the task is overwhelming, at best. For this reason, single parent families are disproportionately represented in the neglect statistics.

Unemployment has also been identified as a common factor among families reported for child mistreatment. The lowered morale and increased financial hardship account for this. With family stress and breakdown come the problems of alcoholism and drug addiction.[3] Addiction problems have been highly correlated with child mistreatment. Whether family breakdown is a cause or a result of addiction is unclear. The two seem to function together. In these ways, society's maltreatment of its poor, minority members contributes to parents' maltreatment of their children.

The problem of child maltreatment is not exclusively one of the poor minority family, however. Increasing numbers of middle and upper income parents are abusing and neglecting their children. Many of the causes are the same as those mentioned for the poor minority families. Addictions, severe emotional stress, and lack of time and interest in children caused by the need for personal strivings may lead individuals to mistreat their children. The tendency remains, however, to look the other way and let it go. These people need help and are even less likely to get it because their middle class status protects them from agency intervention. The statistics are derived from minority families with previous involvements with social agencies.

[2]Ibid., p. 51.

[3]Ibid.

Indicators of Child Maltreatment

The Child

Visible bruises or signs that the child is not being cared for are the most obvious indicators of child abuse and neglect. Any extreme emotional behavior or dramatic change in the emotional state of the child indicates that there is a problem. Although child abuse or neglect is only one potential problem, it should not be overlooked when making the initial assessment.

The Parent

When a parent belittles the child, sees the child as bad, or generally seems to lack concern for or interest in the child, there is reason to suspect child abuse or neglect. Often the parent sees the child as unloving or unappreciative of the parent's efforts. When the parent feels continuously drained and overwhelmed, neglectful or abusive behavior often follow out of desperation.

Several of these indicators in conjunction with each other suggest a potentially dangerous situation. If the child is not presently being mistreated, preventive actions should be taken, for mistreatment may soon occur.

Effects of Child Abuse and Neglect

Child abuse and neglect affect all aspects of the child's development. Physical injury is often slight; most victims of child abuse suffer nothing more than superficial bruises. In its most severe forms, however, physical abuse can cause brain damage leading to retardation, organ damage, and in some cases, death. Abused children do suffer emotionally, through impaired ego development. This is manifested in many different forms of behavior. The child may exhibit high levels of aggression and show lack of impulse control or may be passive and withdrawn. An abused/neglected child suffers cognitive impairment as evidenced by slow motor development, significant learning problems, and impaired language development. Abuse and lack of nurturance can cause delays in the development of all age appropriate skills.

Prevention

Primary prevention requires a good social policy for families and children. Adequate family income, decent housing and accessible health care for all are prerequisites in providing the atmosphere for healthful family functioning. Parental isolation is one of the main factors associated with child maltreatment and must be overcome. Relief from child care and socialization for the parents must be made possible. Special programs such as parent education and child socialization serve to enhance family life and decrease the incidence of child mistreatment. For preventive programs to work effectively, attention must focus on the prediction and early identification of families at risk.

Kempe, in his research at the University of Colorado, has been able to assess accurately high risk mother-child relationships through interview and observation of the mother and infant during labor, delivery and the post-partum hospital stay. He was able to identify those most likely to have future problems. He found that intervention significantly reduces the child's risk of injury.[4] (See Tables I, II, III)

Special efforts should be made to make family life education programs available to high risk families. Programs which reduce isolation and provide relief to parents must also include such practical services as babysitting and transportation to function effectively. Such comprehensive programs will contribute to improved family functioning.

TABLE I - WARNING SIGNS

These are <u>indications</u> of possible problems. A high-risk situation is created by varying combinations of these signs, the family's degree of emphasis upon them, and the family's willingness to change. The interviewer must take into consideration the mother's age, culture, and education, as well as observations of her affect and the significance of her feelings. Many of these signs can be observed throughout the prenatal

[4]J. D. Gray, et. al., "Prediction and Prevention of Child Abuse and Neglect," <u>The International Journal</u>, New York, Pergamon Press, 1977, pp. 45-53.

period; they are listed in this order because they are found most commonly at these times.

1a - <u>Observations during the prenatal period</u>

The mother seems overly concerned with the baby's sex or performance.

The mother exhibits denial of the pregnancy (not willing to gain weight, no plans for the baby, refusal to talk about the situation).

This child could be "one too many."

The mother is extremely depressed over the pregnancy.

The mother is very frightened and alone, especially in anticipation of delivery. Careful explanations do not seem to dissipate the fears.

There is lack of support from husband and/or family.

The mother and/or father formerly wanted an abortion or seriously considered relinquishment and have changed their minds.

The parents come from an abusive/neglectful background.

The parents' living situation is overcrowded, isolated, unstable, or is intolerable to them.

They do not have a telephone.

There are no supportive relatives and/or friends.

1b - <u>Observations during delivery</u>

Written form with baby's chart of parent's reaction at birth.

How does the mother LOOK?
What does the mother SAY?
What does the mother DO?

When the father attends delivery, record his reactions as well.

Passive reaction, either verbal or non-verbal: mother doesn't touch, hold, or examine baby, nor talk in affectionate terms or tones about the baby.

Hostile reaction, either verbal or non-verbal: mother makes inappropriate verbalizations, glances, or disparaging remarks about the physical characteristics of the child.

Disappointment over the sex of the baby.

No eye-contact.

Non-supportive interaction between the parents.

If interaction seems dubious, talk to the nurse and doctor involved with delivery for further information.

1c - <u>Observations during the postpartum period</u>

The mother doesn't have fun with the baby.

The mother avoids eye contact with the baby and avoids the direct <u>en face</u> position.

The verbalizations to the infant are negative, demanding, harsh, etc.

Most of the mother's verbalizations to others about the child are negative.

The parents remain disappointed over the sex of the child.

Negative identification of the child: significance of name, who he/she looks like and/or acts like.

The parents have expectations developmentally far beyond the child's capabilities.

The mother is very bothered by crying; it makes her feel hopeless, helpless, or like crying herself.

Feedings: the mother sees the baby as too demanding; she is repulsed by his messiness, or ignores his demands.

Changing diapers is seen as a very negative, repulsive task.

The mother does not comfort the baby when he cries.

The husband's and/or family's reaction to the baby have been negative or non-supportive.

The mother is receiving little or no meaningful support from anyone.

There are sibling rivalry problems or a complete lack of understanding of this possibility.

The husband is very jealous of the baby's drain on mother's time, energy and affection.

The mother lacks control over the situation. She is not involved, nor does she respond to the baby's needs, but relinquishes control to the doctors or nurses.

When attention is focused on the child in her presence, the mother does not see this as something positive for herself.

The mother makes complaints about the baby that cannot be verified.

TABLE II - POSITIVE FAMILY CIRCUMSTANCES

Parents see likable attributes in baby, see baby as separate individual.

Baby is healthy and not too disruptive to parents' lifestyle.

Either parent can rescue the child or relieve the other in a crisis.

Marriage is stable.

Parents have a good friend or relative to turn to, a sound "need-meeting" system.

Parents exhibit coping abilities; i.e., capacity to plan and understand need for adjustments because of new baby.

Mother's intelligence and health are good.

Parents had helpful role models when growing up.

Parents can have fun together and enjoy personal interests or hobbies.

This baby was planned and wanted.

Future birth control is planned.

Father has stable job.

Parents have their own home and stable living conditions.

Father is supportive to mother and involved in care of baby.

TABLE III
SPECIAL WELL-CHILD CARE FOR HIGH-RISK FAMILIES

Promote maternal attachment to the newborn.

Contact the mother by telephone on the second day after discharge.

Provide more frequent office visits.

Give more attention to the mother.

Emphasize nutrition.

Counsel discipline only around accident prevention.

Emphasize accident prevention.

Use compliments rather than criticism.

Accept phone calls at home.

Provide regular home visits by Public Health Nurse or Lay Health Visitor.[5]

[5]Reprinted with permission from Child Abuse and Neglect: The International Journal, Volume I, J.D. Gray, et. al., "Prediction and Prevention of Child Abuse and Neglect," 1977, Pergaman Press Ltd.

FOR STUDY AND DISCUSSION

1. Racial discrimination and class bias in all aspects of life contribute to the problems of child abuse and neglect. Explain this statement.

2. Primary prevention of child maltreatment requires a good social policy for families and children. What features would need to be included in such a policy?

3. Discuss methods for identifying families at risk and potential preventive measures that could be taken.

Student Exercises

These exercises are designed to heighten the student's awareness of sources of family stress and conflict. Exercise 1 challenges students to identify sources of stress which could result in family breakdown. In Exercise 2, students are asked to examine some of the potential family conflicts which may arise from differences of belief among family members.

EXERCISE #1   STRESS BRAINSTORM

MATERIALS: Newsprint and magic markers
                          or
                 Paper and pen or pencil

PROCEDURE:

1. The instructor begins by dividing the class into subgroups of four to seven members. Ask students to join other members of their subgroup in a designated area of the room.

2. The instructor should give a brief description of the activity:

    In today's presentation, we spoke of the negative effects of stress on the familial relationship. We are now going to work together to identify some specific sources of stress in the family. To do this, we will use a brainstorming technique. Many of you are familiar with this strategy, but let me briefly explain the rules for everyone. Your job is to come up with the longest possible list of suggestions in the allotted time. All suggestions are accepted without evaluation; at this point the emphasis is on quantity, not quality. Let yourself be imaginative; some very creative solutions have been developed as an outgrowth of what appeared to be a ridiculous brainstorming suggestion.

3. Distribute newsprint and magic markers or paper and pens or pencils to each group. Ask one member to serve as the recorder. Ask students to practice their brainstorming skills on a sample topic. Their task will be to list all of the sources of stress in their personal lives in two

43

minutes: When do they feel tense? Annoyed?
Anxious? This warm-up exercise is designed to be
enjoyable. The instructor should try to encourage
students to relax and have fun.

4. Allow two to three minutes for the practice exercise. When lists are completed, ask each group
to share the information.

5. Once the instructor is sure that all students are
familiar with the technique, have each group begin
the major brainstorming list. Ask students to
list as many sources of family stress as they can.
Note that this stress may come from the adult
couple's relationship, from the society, and/or
from the children.

6. Students should be given five to ten minutes to
complete their lists. There may be brief silences
in some groups; this is to be expected. When all
groups appear to have exhausted their resources,
the instructor should signal the end of the brainstorming and return the focus to the full group.

PROCESSING:

1. Ask the recorder from each subgroup to share the
information from the group list. If lists are on
newsprint, the instructor may choose to hang the
lists on the wall after each group has had an
opportunity to report its results.

2. Use the information from these lists to generate
class discussion. Questions might include the
following:

   a. What did you learn by doing this activity?

   b. Which of these stresses do you view as most
   dangerous for the family?

   c. Which type of family stress do you see as most
   debilitating -- inner family stress or outside
   stress?

   d. Why do you think so many families seem to
   ignore rising stress levels?

   e. How much stress is "normal stress."

f.   What do you think should be done to reduce
     family stress levels?

g.   How do you respond when your personal stress
     level gets too high?

EXERCISE #2   FAMILY RANK ORDERS

MATERIALS: Newsprint and markers
                        or
              Blackboard

PROCEDURE:

1. The instructor should begin by dividing the class
    into triads. Ask triad members to sit together
    facing each other.

2. The instructor should give directions to students:

        This activity is designed to help you explore
        some of your personal beliefs and values
        about family life. I will give you a series
        of questions with three possible responses
        for each question. Please rank order the al-
        ternative responses according to your pre-
        ferences, noting your first, second, and third
        choice. Once you have ranked your choices,
        please share your responses with the other two
        members of your small group. Try to explain
        the reasons for your rankings.

3. The instructor should select four or five questions
    from the list of topics. Allow approximately five
    minutes for each question. Read the question and
    the alternative responses to the group one at a
    time. You may find it helpful to write key words
    from the response choices on a newsprint or black-
    board. After each question, give each student a
    chance to report responses to other triad members.

    NOTE: The following topics offer a fairly wide
    range of complexity. Some questions ask for simple
    straight-forward responses; others pose
    more subtle and difficult questions. A balanced
    blend of simple and complex topics is recommended.

45

FAMILY RANK ORDER TOPICS

1. In which environment would you choose to raise your family?

   _____ rural

   _____ suburban

   _____ urban

2. Which potential family problem would be most stressful for you?

   _____ serious illness

   _____ serious financial problems

   _____ serious relationship problems

3. What do you see as the most challenging task of parents?

   _____ providing physical nurturance

   _____ providing emotional support

   _____ guiding moral development

4. Where would you like to have your parents or in-laws living?

   _____ within walking distance

   _____ within 50 miles

   _____ more than 50 miles away

5. If you thought that your neighbors were mistreating their child, what would you do?

   _____ report it to the authorities

   _____ discuss your concern with the parents

   _____ overlook it

6. What is the most important ingredient in a good family relationship?

    _____ trust

    _____ flexibility

    _____ intimacy

7. What would you be most likely to choose as a family activity?

    _____ hiking

    _____ general family discussion

    _____ family outing to the circus

8. What is the most threatening problem facing the American family in this decade?

    _____ breakdown of the family structure

    _____ economic pressures

    _____ decline in social services

PROCESSING:

The instructor may choose to ask a few topical questions after students have completed their discussion of each item. A summary discussion at the end of the activity would also be appropriate. Summary questions might include the following:

1. Which questions were easiest for you to answer?

2. Which questions gave you some difficulty?

3. How similar were the response patterns within your group? What might this suggest?

4. How do you think your answers might differ from those of your future clients?

5. How would you respond if you learned that your client's views were very different from your own?

6. What did you learn by doing this activity?

References

Bakan, D., Slaughter of the Innocents, San Francisco, CA, Jossey-Bass, 1971.

Chase, N.F., A Child is Being Beaten, New York, McGraw Hill, 1976.

Eberling, N.B. (ed), Child Abuse: Treatment and Intervention, Acton, Mass., Publishing Sciences Group, Inc., 1975.

Fontana, V., The Maltreated Child

Fontana, V., Somewhere a Child is Crying, New York, Macmillan Publishing Co., Inc., 1973.

Gelles, R.J., The Violent Home, Beverly Hills, CA, Sage Publications, 1972.

Gil, D., Violence Against Children, Cambridge, Mass., Harvard University Press, 1970.

Giovananni, J.M., Defining Child Abuse, New York, Free Press, 1979.

Helfer, R., The Battered Child, Chicago, Ill., University of Chicago Press, 1974.

Helfer, R.E. and Kempe, C.H., Child Abuse and Neglect-The Family and the Community, Cambridge, Mass., Ballinger Publishing Co., 1976

Inglis, R., Sins of the Fathers, New York, St. Martins Press, 1978.

Kempe, C., Child Abuse and Neglect-The International Journal, Pergamon Press, 1977.

Kempe, C., Helping the Battered Child and his Family, Lippincott, 1972.

Martin, H.(ed), The Abused Child, Cambridge, Mass., Ballinger Publishing Co., 1976.

Martin, J.P., Violence and the Family, New York, J. Wiley & Sons, Inc., 1978.

Viano, E. (ed), <u>Child Abuse and Neglect-Victimology,</u>
<u>International Journal</u>, Washington, D.C., 1977.

Young, L., <u>Wednesdays Children</u>, New York, McGraw Hill,
1964.

Periodicals

Besharov, D.J. & S.H., "Why do Parents Harm Their
Children"? <u>National Council of Jewish Women</u>, Winter,
1977.

Dean, D., "Emotional Abuse of Children," <u>Children</u>
<u>Today</u>, July/August, 1979.

Fontana, V.J., "Child Abuse-Symptom of a Violent
Society," <u>National Council of Jewish Women</u>, Winter,
1977.

Giovananni, J.M., "Parental Mistreatment: Perpetrators
and Victims," <u>Journal of Marriage and the Family</u>, 33
(4), November 1971, 649-57.

Gaines, R., Sandgeand, A., Green, "Etiological Factors
in Child Maltreatment," <u>Journal of Abnormal Psychology</u>,
87 (5): 531-40, 1978.

Sussman, A.N., "Keeping Records on Suspected Child
Abuse," <u>National Council of Jewish Women</u>, Winter, 1977.

Theisen, W.M., "What Next in Child Abuse Policy?
Improving the Knowledge Base," <u>Child Welfare</u>, 57 (7),
415-21, 1978.

<u>Children Today</u>, May/June, 1975.

Audio Visual Materials

<u>Violence in the Family</u>, Human Relations Media, 175
Tompkins Ave., Pleasantville, NY 10570.

CHAPTER IV

CHILD NEGLECT

"The neglected child lives with and is neglected by his parents. His plight differs from that of the deprived child who has been deprived of his parents and is therefore free to forage for the attention of others. The neglected child lives in the solitude of a family prison."[1]

The problem of child neglect is one of growing concern in this nation. Cases of child neglect far outnumber any other form of child maltreatment.

Definitions

Child neglect refers to the failure of a responsible adult to provide the proper level of care with respect to food, clothing, shelter, hygiene, medical attention, guidance, emotional support, and supervision. It also encompasses those situations where the parent is unable to provide necessary emotional and physical nurturance, stimulation, and/or encouragement to the child at various states in the child's development. Neglect inhibits optimal functioning and affects overall development.

In those cases where a child's basic physical needs are not being met, neglect is generally quite easy to identify. However, when a child is deprived of experiences that develop feelings of being loved, wanted, and secure, identification and subsequent intervention become more difficult. Whether child neglect results from acts of omission or commission, the problems of the neglected child represent a serious area of concern in our society.

Characteristics

Child neglect is a multi-causal, chronic problem. Child neglect is often lumped together with the more commonly discussed but less prevalent problem of child abuse. The literature and government legislation

[1]"Proceedings of the Conference on the Care of Dependent Children," Washington, D.C., 60th Congress, 2nd Session, January 1909.

treat them as one problem. In reality, they are two separate entities with different causative factors and intervention implications.

Child neglect is more often associated with extreme poverty and social stress than any other form of mistreatment. This social factor must be considered when working toward a solution of an isolated family, as well as when examining American social policy to assess its effects on family functioning. However, emotional neglect is also found in middle and upper income families.

It is difficult to define "proper level of care" or minimum standards. Therefore, the assessment of a family is a subjective one. Cultural influences must also be understood and accepted. Behavior that appears to be neglectful may be normal within a particular community. Each case must be examined individually within the context of the total family and cultural situation, in terms of what is and is not being done for the child and how the child is doing. Society's minimum standards remain, however. There are times when the values and norms of the family are at odds with those of society. Intervention is necessary to bring care to an acceptable level.

It is often difficult to differentiate the behavior of an emotionally neglected child from that of an emotionally disturbed child. The symptoms may appear to be the same. Neglect may be the cause of the emotional disturbance. Examination of the total situation is essential for accurate assessment. Emotional disturbance can be caused by many other factors than neglect, including mental illness, autism, and childhood schizophrenia.

The Parent

The types of personalities observed most frequently among neglecting parents are as follows:

    A. Apathetic - futile - schizoid
    B. Impulse ridden
    C. Mentally Retarded - I.Q. 68-83
    D. Reactive depression

E. Psychotic[2]

Apathetic Parent

The apathetic, futile parent shows signs that
are difficult to differentiate from those of
depression. Here, the parent does remain with
the child, but has little motivation or ability
to carry out the parental role. The numbness
and the sense that nothing is worth doing and
that nothing can ever change make this parent
a difficult one to mobilize. Poor object relations characterize this parent. The situation is long-standing and chronic.

Impulse Ridden Parent

The impulse ridden parent is restless and
rebellious. This parent cannot tolerate
stress or frustration and responds by irrespon-
sibility, "taking off" on an impulse in search
of excitment or change. This parent is often
completely adequate and competent in most
areas and the neglect is episodic. This type
of parent tends to be manipulative, especially
of anyone who offers help.

Mentally Retarded Parent

The mentally retarded parent is neglectful by
the definition of the parent's inadequacy.
The problems of illiteracy, telling time,
remembering dates, managing money, etc., make
it impossible for this parent to keep appoint-
ments for the child, or provide the necessary
opportunities for the child to develop. This
type of parent is suggestible and vulnerable
to being exploited. The concreteness and
rigidity of the thinking make it difficult for
this type of parent to show good judgment in
rearing of the child.

---

[2]Polansky, N.A., "Prevalent Types of Neglectful
Mothers," Child Neglect: Understanding and Reaching
the Parent, 1972, Child Welfare League of America,
Inc., pp. 21-53

Reactive Depressed Parent

The parent in a reactive depression is immobilized by the depression. It is seen in a person who previously functioned as an adequate parent, whose behavior has changed. This depressive state is in response to a trauma or loss. The parent is unable to care for personal needs, let alone the needs of the child.

Psychotic Parent

The psychotic parent has lost contact with reality. This is exhibited through bizarre behavior, thought disorders, delusions, or hallucinations. This parent must be immediately referred for psychiatric help.

The neglecting parent is a "victim." This parent acts as a child immersed in self-need and has difficulty responding to the needs of others. Many neglecting parents see themselves as stupid, inadequate, and failures. They have difficulty handling responsibility, often have defective judgment, and are usually emotionally detached from their children. The neglecting parent's basic needs were not met as a child and have remained unmet as an adult. This parent identifies with the negative parenting from the family of origin, causing the child care to be poor. These parents can be helped with social work intervention.

The Child

The neglected child is often a detached and depressed person with little motivation or incentive for action. Because so many of the child's needs have not been met, this child has difficulty trusting others. The child is a follower and very suggestible, searching for direction and fulfillment. The neglected child, with proper intervention, can be very responsive and will no longer show flattened affect.

Nonorganic Failure to Thrive

Nonorganic failure to thrive is the most severe form of infant neglect. It is defined as those below the fifth percentile on the national pediatric growth charts and is caused by the lack of appropriate

maternal-infant attachment in the first year of life.
The result is a failure to grow, gain, and thrive, frequently causing malnutrition which curtails the normal
increase in brain cellularity. With increasing age,
permanent damage results.

This dysfunction is very difficult to treat in
both the parent and child and often results in the
death of the child. At best, the child will lag in
development. The mother is most often inadequate,
lacking in basic child care knowledge or suffering
from a psychiatric disorder.

Intervention with a Neglecting Parent

The neglecting parent has difficulty in making
emotional attachments. The parent is not possessive
of the child. This parent, therefore, may be more
inclined to let the child be placed than to want to
work on changing. This is the most negative factor
in the prognosis.

A neglecting parent can benefit from a positive
relationship with a social worker. This parent has
probably never had a relationship where the parent was
the main object of concern. An accepting relationship,
valuing this parent as an individual, does much to
enhance the sense of self. The neglecting parent, as
a child, values anything concrete that is given. A cup
of coffee, help with any chores or the children, or any
form of diversion provide the much needed relief from
the routine. For the neglecting parent, life is a
problem with many failures. The social work experience
must provide immediate success for this parent. The
worker can then help to build on small successes.

The social worker is a role model for this parent.
With the increasing identification with the worker,
the parent can develop new values and decrease the
negative identification with the parenting of the family
of origin. Social isolation is characteristic of the
neglecting parent. Any attempts to reduce this isolation through groups within the agency or involvement
in activities within the community will be helpful.
The intervention process may be a long and slow one.
The focus must remain on the parent as an individual
in need in order to be effective.

Early Identification and Prevention of Neglecting Parents

A history of neglect of the parent, as a child, or of other children in the family should alert the agency to the possibility of the process continuing. An especially young parent immersed in poverty, isolated, and lacking in support systems presents as a high risk parent. A child who appears to be lacking in adequate basic care may be neglected.

An agency worker must remain aware that these factors may indicate neglect or a tendency to neglect. Intervention in the form of education in parenting skills and the family life education programs have been demonstrated as effective preventive measures. Involvement in activities to reduce social isolation are important as well. Referral for supplementary income and services such as homemakers and day-care can relieve the family's life pressures and may either reduce or prevent child neglect.

FOR STUDY AND DISCUSSION

1. Child neglect is often associated with extreme poverty and social stress. Discuss the implications of this statement with respect to individual family intervention. In what ways does American social policy promote child neglect?

2. What is nonorganic failure to thrive? Discuss the factors of significance in the prevention of this problem.

3. The line between acceptable cultural difference in child rearing styles and a condition of neglect is often a fine one. Discuss the conditions that would enable one to identify a neglectful situation requiring intervention.

Student Exercises

These exercises focus on neglect. Exercise 1 uses a role play situation in which students are asked to explore their personal responses to neglect. Exercise 2 presents a hypothetical case study of a neglecting family. Students are asked to identify specific problems and recommend intervention strategies.

EXERCISE #1   ARE WE NEGLECTORS?

MATERIALS: A copy of the role play instructions for each of the two participants

PROCEDURE:

1.   The instructor begins by selecting two students to participate in a role play. Role play participants may be appointed or volunteers may be requested.

2.   The instructor gives each participating student a copy of the respective role descriptions.

3.   While the role play participants are familiarizing themselves with their roles, the instructor explains the observers' role to other members of the class.

> The scene which you are about to watch will include some subtle examples of neglect. You will not take an active role in this situation. You are simply asked to observe the process of the interaction, watching for significant verbal and non-verbal responses which occur as the role play progresses.

4.   The instructor should ask role play participants to begin. Allow the scenario to continue to a natural termination.

PROCESSING:

1.   Return the students to a full group discussion of the topic. Begin by asking the role play participants to share their reactions to the activity.

2.   Ask remaining class members to share any observations which they may have made while the role play was in progress. Encourage observers to identify

any verbal or non-verbal clues which suggested
neglecting behavior.

3. Some possible questions for general discussion:

    a. Do you think that this interaction can be
        categorized as neglect? Why or why not?

    b. Can you recall similar experiences from your
        own life? How did you feel?

    c. What are some typical responses which one
        might exhibit in a neglecting situation?

    d. Can you think of potential situations where
        you might unintentionally neglect your clients?

    e. What can a social worker do to avoid neglecting
        reactions to clients?

    f. What have you learned from this activity?

NEGLECT ROLE PLAY

Role #1:   <u>Anne</u>

You are a field work instructor awaiting a regular
visit from Sally, one of your social work students.
Sally is a talented student, but she has been
having some difficulty with one particular client.
You have given her help with the case and you are
confident that she will eventually be successful.

You've also applied to graduate school, hoping to
be accepted into a doctoral program. While you
are waiting for Sally to come in for her regular
supervisory appointment, you get a letter from
your first choice school. You anxiously open the
letter and learn that you have been accepted.
You're overjoyed and you're dying to share your
good news with anyone and everyone. You're glad
that Sally is due in your office momentarily so
that you'll have someone to tell.

The role play begins as Sally enters the room.

Role #2:   <u>Sally</u>

You are a social work student. You've been very
successful in your classwork and most of your field
work cases have been progressing reasonably well.
The one exception is Harry, a client who has been
exhibiting some resistance.

Harry was referred to your agency by probation.
He had been incarcerated for eighteen months.
Since his release, he had experienced aimlessness
and mild depression. He has reported feeling overwhelmed by the tasks involved in re-establishing
himself in the community. You have been working
with Harry for two months. You've conferred with
Anne, your field work instructor, many times on
this case. She's been supportive and helpful,
frequently suggesting possible new approaches to
use with Harry. You've appreciated her guidance,
and yet, you've continued to feel frustrated and
unsure of yourself.

This past week when Harry came to see you, he
finally had good news. Harry had found a job.
He reported that he enjoyed work and felt more

self-confidence. You're thrilled for Harry and
for yourself. You can hardly wait to share the
good news with Anne. You're particularly anxious
to discuss your future interventions with Harry.

The role play begins as you enter Anne's office.

EXERCISE #2   CASE STUDY OF NEGLECT

MATERIALS: Copies of case study for each student

                 Paper and pens

                 Newsprint and markers or blackboard

PROCEDURE:

1. The instructor should begin by dividing the class
    into subgroups with three to six members. It is
    desirable to have at least three subgroups for
    this activity, so subgroup size should be deter-
    mined accordingly.

2. The instructor explains the activity to students:

        Today we are going to examine a hypothetical
        case study which centers on a neglecting
        family. Each of you will receive a copy of
        the vital information in this case. Once you
        have familiarized yourself with the particu-
        lars of the case, you will be asked to work
        together as a group to develop a "PIP" or
        Preliminary Intervention Plan. Your plan
        should include the following information:

    a. Identification of <u>specific problems</u> in the
        family system.

    b. Recommendations for <u>specific intervention
        strategies</u> which could be used with this
        family.

    c. A detailed description of the <u>social worker's
        task</u> which you would perform.

    d. Comprehensive list of outside <u>agency referrals</u>
        which might be used for this family.

    NOTE: Key words which are underlined should be
           listed on a newsprint or blackboard. You will
           have about fifteen minutes to work on this
           task. Each group will then be asked to pre-
           sent its "PIP" to the class.

3. Hand out student copies of the case study. Allow
    fifteen to twenty minutes for group work. When

time has elapsed, reconvene small groups for full class discussion.

PROCESSING:

1. Ask one member from each subgroup to report the information from the group's Preliminary Intervention Plan. If you are working with a large class, a full report may be too time consuming. If so, focus on information from Section B. It would be advisable to develop a composite list of specific suggestions on newsprints or on the blackboard.

2. Some possible questions for discussion:

   a. Which part of this task was easiest for you? Why?

   b. Which part of this task was most difficult for you? Why?

   c. What factors will contribute to the success or failure of your "PIP"?

   d. As you discussed this case, were you conscious of any feelings which you were experiencing? How did you feel toward the mother? The children? Yourself?

   e. How do you think you would feel if you were actually assigned to this case?

   f. What have you learned from this activity?

CASE STUDY OF NEGLECT

This is a lower income Black family with a long history of agency involvement. The case has been opened and closed numerous times. The last time it was reopened because the mother abandoned her children on the doorstep of a woman's house. The children were picked up by their grandmother who has limited intelligence and is deaf. The children had been in their grandmother's care for two months.

The mother has recently spent one month in jail. She is now out on bail. She is also six months pregnant. There are three children in the family; a girl of seven, a boy of four who has cancer and needs constant medical attention, and a girl of two who has no verbal skills and no teeth. The father(s) of the children is (are) unknown.

The case was reopened when the school reported the apparent neglect of the oldest child. She was coming to school with an unkempt appearance and inadequate clothing. She was often lethargic and complained of hunger.

The initial assessment took place at a run-down hotel where the family was living after a fire had forced them out of the grandmother's home. During the initial visit, the social worker found deplorable conditions. The motel room reeked with the odor of urine. It was cluttered with debris including cigarette butts, beer bottles, and spoiled foods. It was extremely dark.

During the initial visit, the children were timid and withdrawn and the social worker observed the youngest child playing with the electrical socket. The mother was passive, but not uncooperative. She paid little attention to the children and her responses were vague and apathetic.

Preliminary Intervention Plan Guidelines

1. Identify specific problems in this family system.

2. Make recommendations for specific interventions to be used with this family.

3. Outline tasks which a social worker would perform.

4. Identify necessary outside agency referrals.

63

References

Cartwell, H., "Standards of Child Neglect," October, 1978.

Jacobucci, L., "Casework Treatment of the Neglectful Mother," Social Casework, April, 1965.

Polansky, N. et. al., Profile of Neglect: A Survey of the State of Knowledge of Child Neglect, U.S. Department of HEW, 1975.

Selected Readings on Child Neglect, U.S. Department of HEW, January, 1980.

Whiting, L., "Defining Emotional Neglect," Children Today, January, February, 1976.

Audio Visual Materials

The Neglected, Audio Visual Services, The Pennsylvania State University, University Park, PA 16802

Night Children, Audio Visual Services, The Pennsylvania State University, University Park, PA 16802

64

CHAPTER V

CHILD ABUSE

"It would seem that among both animals and humans, the instinct to nourish and the impulse to maim and destroy exist side by side. . . Indeed, although child abuse - from wounding and torture to selling and abandonment to outright murder - has received an unusual amount of attention in the last few years, the maltreatment of children is as old as humankind."[1]

Child abuse is the number one killer of children under three years of age.

Definitions of Child Abuse

Child abuse is the intentional, nonaccidental use of physical force aimed at hurting the child. The parent is immersed in the act of punishing without regard for its cause or purpose. It is punishment, divorced from discipline. In its severest form, child abuse results in broken bones, burns, ruptured organs, or death. The largest percentage of abuse is mild abuse. An outside observer may feel that the behavior is excessive without being horrible. The parent feels that it is just punishment and within parental rights. This gray area poses problems to protective service workers with respect to identification and effective intervention.

Characteristics of Child Abuse

Child abuse is less associated with poverty and social stress and more related to psychopathology than child neglect. There is growing concern about child abuse in middle and upper income families. However, the poor, minority family remains over-represented in the abuse statistics of the police and social agencies. The question of whether this is due to the increased tendency to report and act when the poor minority family is involved and to overlook the middle class family remains unanswered. The private physician is also less likely to identify and report abuse than a physician working in a clinic or public hospital.

---

[1]N.F. Chase, _A Child is Being Beaten_, New York, McGraw Hill, 1976, p. 10.

In many families, one child is the target of the aggression. The parent may identify personal negative qualities or negative qualities of the spouse or ex-spouse in the child. Often, the victim is a difficult child to handle. Handicapped children are over represented in the abuse statistics. In other cases, it appears that one child is the victim of the abuse. However, if this child is removed from the home, another child is chosen as the replacement target for the aggression. This raises the question as to whether the abuse causes the child to be difficult or whether the difficulty causes the abuse.

In a two-parent family, often one parent is the aggressor and the other is a victim. The nonabusing parent who may be competent in other aspects of life may behave as a prisoner within the home. The individual's passivity is based on fear of the abusing spouse. The passive parent feels personally threatened and is unable to protect the child. The parent remains in the situation, unable to leave, and defends the aggressor to the family or to outside authorities.

An abusing parent is angry. The child takes the brunt of the parent's anger. The child represents weakness. The child is seen as dependent on and a possession of the parent. Role reversal is a concept associated with child abuse. The needy, hurting parent looks to the child for the love and care the parent craves and has never received. The parent's expectations of the child are unrealistic and age inappropriate. The parent strikes out in anger when the child is unable to meet the parent's needs.

Child abuse is a problem of ambivalence. As angry and hurtful as the parent is toward the child, the parent is equally attached to and involved with the child. The parent is possessive of the child to the point of preventing the child from outside relationships and activities. This may be based on the fear that the child would talk about the abuse within the family and become aware of the differences of behavior between this and other families.

The Parent

The abusive parent, like the neglecting parent, has not had dependency and nurturance needs met. This parent may have been abused as a child. The parent presents an image of low self-esteem. The parent's abusive behavior is caused by inadequate coping skills.

Social isolation is characteristic of the abusive parent. Even the middle class mother who appears to have much going for her may be very isolated. A close look at her involvement or lack of involvement in various activities shows her to be on the outside. The abusive parent has difficulty in forming close relationships. This parent, therefore, lacks effective support systems.

Abusive behavior is often in response to a life crisis. An isolated crisis may lead to an isolated abusive episode. A crisis-ridden way of life may develop into a chronically abusive situation. Familial stress, such as marital problems or economic stress involving unemployment, inadequate housing, and general impoverishment are common precursors to abusive behavior. The single parent with no one to share the burdens of child rearing has an increased tendency to abuse the child.

The abusive parent is unable to care for, protect and empathize with the child. This may be because the parent lacked a nurturing role model. The parent may lack normal developmental knowledge and have unrealistic expectations of the child. The child may have a handicap or developmental disability causing the child to demand a great deal and give little in return. Whatever the reason or reasons, the parent is overwhelmed, resentful, and unable to cope with the parenting role.

The abusing parent is often suspicious, presenting bizarre behavior with a disconnected quality and poor judgment. Although this parent does not usually consciously desire to harm the child, the parent commits the acts and does not feel guilty. The parent blames the child and sees the abusing behavior as a natural response to the child.

The Child

Abused children see themselves as generally bad. Just as the parent blames the child, these children blame themselves for everything that has happened to them. An abused child's behavior may take a variety of forms. The child may be overly compliant and

and passive, trying to avoid punishment at all costs.
On the other hand, this child may be extremely aggressive and demanding. The child may use violence to
obtain attention. The violence is erratic and unpre-
dictable. Some children grow up quickly, acting as
little parents, trying to respond to their parent's
attempts at role reversal. Others are extremely imma-
ture and babyish. This wide range of behavior makes it
impossible to diagnose child abuse from the child's
behavior alone.

Emotional Abuse of the Child

Emotional abuse involves the destruction or impairment of the child's self-esteem. Because it does not
involve bruises and broken bones, it is the hardest
form of child maltreatment to define, and identify,
and prove. It is extremely difficult to make an effective case for legal action. Emotional abuse may have
deeper, longer range effects on the child than physical
abuse. Personalities do not heal as easily as bones.

Emotional abuse can be seen in a variety of forms
and is indicative of family and relationship problems.
It is the penalizing of the child for showing normal,
positive behavior as in exploration and assertiveness.
The parent may penalize the child for showing signs of
positive self-esteem or for appropriate developmental
and interpersonal skills. Verbal abuse and verbal
threat also constitute emotional abuse.

The effects of emotional abuse can be devastating.
It can result in permanent damage to the self-esteem
and self-confidence of the child. Emotional abuse
impairs the inquiring nature of the child and inhibits
the growth and learning. An emotionally abused child
rarely shows signs of spontaneity or enthusiasm for
living.

Intervention in Cases of Child Abuse

Problems of child abuse are more difficult to
treat than those of neglect. These parents do not
trust, are fearful of close relationships, and do not
want to discuss themselves or their past. Abusive
parents rarely become voluntarily involved or remain
involved with an agency. Much of protective service
work is with hostile clients and is based on the legal
and social sanctions of the agency. Effective work

68

with abusive parents is long term with slow gains and many setbacks.

When engaging the abusive parent, the worker must use authority. A clear, firm, honest statement of purpose hastens the process of developing trust. While the attitude is direct and firm, it should be supportive, not punitive. The goal is to help the parents to improve child rearing and self-control without punishing the parents. One of the biggest obstacles is the worker's overidentification with the child and anger toward the parents. Awareness of personal feelings will enable the worker to overcome this obstacle. The emphasis of the intervention is optimistic, presenting the sense that people can and do change. One can develop self-control.

Individual, family and group intervention can be effective with abusing parents. Individual intervention should focus on concrete goals and should avoid highly confrontive and personal issues. Family intervention is aimed at developing new interactional patterns within the family. Group interaction is also highly effective. The self-help group, Parents Anonymous, claims to provide the least threatening and most effective intervention for its members. Although it began as a voluntary organization, courts are increasingly mandating parents to participate in the program. Agency groups focused on member interaction and support or child development and child rearing education also serve a valuable purpose. A combination of approaches used in conjunction with each other meet arising family needs and provide the most useful approach to problem resolution.

Early Identification and Prevention

A parent who was abused as a child or one who has previously demonstrated abusive behavior is a high risk parent. A child with a handicap or developmental disability may strain family resources and supports and has an increased chance of being abused. The existence of psychiatric or substance addiction problems in families have also been highly correlated with child abuse. A change in the conditions of a high risk family increases the possibility of child abuse. A change in marital status, the loss of a job, a health problem, the return of a previously placed child, a move, or the birth of a new baby all can push the vulnerable family over the edge. Awareness of these factors can enable the agency to intervene prior to the actual abuse. Helping the family to connect with available resources such as therapeutic day care, homemaker services, counseling centers, and Parents Anonymous may prevent the abuse from occurring.

Family Life education programs should be available to everyone. They must be located in accessible places, be free of charge, and have babysitting services available. This may do much to improve the quality of family life in America.

FOR STUDY AND DISCUSSION

1. Discuss the similarities and differences that characterize abusive and neglectful parents.

2. What is emotional abuse? Using examples from your work or personal experiences, describe the effects it can have on the child.

3. Early identification is a key factor in the solution of child abuse problems. Discuss some of the conditions that would cause one to suspect child abuse.

Student Exercises

These exercises are designed to heighten the student's awareness of the difficult issues involved in child abuse intervention. In Exercise 1, students are asked to examine their personal responses to six different forms of abusive behavior. Exercise 2 presents a case study of abuse which repeats the format developed in the previous chapter.

EXERCISE #1   THE ABUSERS

MATERIALS: Blackboard or newsprint

               Copies of sheet with six scenarios
               (one for each student)

PROCEDURE:

1.   The instructor should begin by explaining the
     class activity:

          Child abuse presents a difficult and demanding
          challenge to the social worker. The plight of
          the abused child has received a great deal of
          attention recently; yet, there has been very
          little attention paid to the special skills
          which are required to intervene effectively
          in cases of child abuse. Before entering the
          emotionally charged arena of child abuse, it
          may be wise for us to examine those personal
          feelings or prejudices which relate to the
          various forms of abusive behavior. To begin
          the process today, I will present a series of
          hypothetical abusive situations and ask you to
          respond to them.

2.   Instructor presents the following situations,
     placing the name of each client on the board or
     newsprint.

          Imagine yourself as a social worker who spe-
          cializes in abuse cases. Your caseload in-
          cludes the following six cases:

     a.   Alvin: Alvin is a middle class father of four
          children. He has a history of severe episodic
          drinking. Last Friday Alvin learned that he
          had been passed over for a promotion which he

71

was counting on to help pay for his family's ever-inflating bills. He left work and headed straight for the corner pub to drown his frustration. The more he drank, the angrier he became. When he finally arrived home at 9:00 p.m., he was close to rage. He was met at the door by his seven year old son who took one look at his father, turned to his mother and said, "Oh no! Dad's been drinking again." With his son's comment, Alvin lost control, struck the boy, and knocked him against a table and onto the floor. The boy screamed; he had a broken arm.

b. Beverly: Beverly is a single parent and a controller. She has a perfectly balanced checkbook, an immaculate house, and a nine year old daughter who always looks like she's just stepped out of an exclusive children's shop. Beverly keeps a close watch over her daughter's activities, a very close watch. With the exception of the six hours a day when her daughter is required to attend school, she is never more than a few feet away from mother's protective wing. Beverly believes that the other neighborhood children are wild and ill mannered, so she discourages any visits by her daughter's peers. As a result, the young girl has virtually no friends and she's developing phobic reactions to any situation which threatens to take her out of her mother's sight.

c. Christine: Christine is the mother of three young children. As an only child herself, she was raised in a family system with clear limits and boundaries. With her own children, she's extremely strict and frequently exhibits her belief in the old adage, "spare the rod and spoil the child." She is particularly sensitive to the bickering which goes on among her children. After one warning, she goes for her trusty belt to make sure that the noise and teasing will stop. Her punishment often results in bruised arms and legs and, occasionally, in broken skin and bleeding. She's the first one to tell you that her discipline also puts a stop to the misbehavior of her children.

d. Dan: Dan is the classic high school jock who
    had visions of a future career in professional
    sports. He never quite made it. His son is a
    strong, healthy lad of twelve who has little
    or no interest in following along in Dad's
    sneakers! He'd much rather spend his leisure
    time with his friends and his guitar than a
    basketball or a baseball bat. Dan will not be
    deterred in his efforts, however. He expects
    that his son will make first string on the
    school basketball team and serve as catcher
    for the Babe Ruth League allstars. Dan's son
    is afraid to express his true feelings. In-
    stead he vents his dismay through poor per-
    formance in school, extreme moodiness, and
    frequent bouts with mysterious illnesses. Dan
    is not concerned about these "minor" problems.
    He just wants to be sure that his son will
    eventually win a sports scholarship to college
    and will go on to gain the fame and fortune
    which eluded his dad.

e. Ernest: Ernest is the father of two children.
    His youngest son was born with a severe handi-
    cap which has affected his mobility and motor
    control. Ernest's wife has insisted that
    every effort be made to get the best medical
    care for their son. For the past three years,
    the family has been involved in an intensive
    experimental program which requires five hours
    of physical therapy for their son daily.
    Ernest reluctantly helped with the therapy for
    two years despite his reservations about the
    value of the treatment. During this time span,
    the boy showed little sign of real progress,
    but his condition remained fairly stable.

    Within the last year, Ernest has become more
    and more resistant to the time commitment in-
    volved in the physical therapy. Ernest's wife
    cannot manage all of the therapy program her-
    self. As a result of the decrease in thera-
    peutic activity, their son is beginning to
    show some signs of physical deterioration.
    Ernest contends that this is inevitable and
    that the reduction in his involvement is
    inconsequential.

f. Flora: Flora is a whiner. She's a classic

overworked and under-appreciated mother.
Flora's favorite diversion is the soap operas;
her greatest nemesis is housework. She has a
solution to the housework problem. The solution is her ten year old son who is expected
to spend his time after school and on Saturday
cleaning up the messy house which Flora is too
oppressed to manage. From her seat in front
of the TV, Flora gives the orders - make the
beds, clean the bathroom, do the dishes, vacuum
the carpets, wash the clothes, set the table,
and put the TV dinners in the oven. When
everything is done, her son is free to play.
Unfortunately, he has no energy left.

3. Instructor distributes worksheets to each student
and gives the following instructions:

As a child abuse social worker, you strive to
be warm and empathetic. Sometimes it may be
very difficult. If these were your clients,
how would you rank them in terms of "empathiz-
ability"? How easy or difficult would you find
it to be accepting and non-judgmental with
these clients? Please rank each of your clients on your "empathizability" scale: #1
indicates the client whom you could accept
most easily, #6 indicates the client whom you
would find most difficult to accept.

PROCESSING:

1. Ask students to find a partner and share their
lists.

2. The instructor may want to ask students to report
their rankings and develop a composite class list
on the board or a newsprint. Such a list would
allow the class to look at patterns or response
and similarities and differences in reactions.

3. Possible discussion topics:

a. How did you feel as I was going through the
list of abuse cases?

b. How easy or difficult did you find it to complete the task?

c. How would you explain the numerous different rankings in the class?

d. What criteria did you use to rank the cases?

e. What did your personal responses tell you about yourself as a potential child abuse social worker?

f. What could you do to increase your "empathiz-ability"?

g. Would you enjoy a position as a child abuse social worker? Why or why not?

"EMPATHIZABILITY SCALE"

DIRECTIONS: Please rank the following six clients in terms of your ability to respond to them with acceptance and support.

#1 - Client whom you could accept most easily

#6 - Client whom you would find most difficult to accept.

_____ Alvin: Heavy drinker who broke his son's arm

_____ Beverly: Controlling mother who protects her daughter

_____ Christine: Firm disciplinarian who takes the belt to her children

_____ Dan: Would-be athletic father who pushes his son into sports

_____ Ernest: Father of handicapped son who refuses to continue physical therapy

_____ Flora: Mother who overloads her son with housework while she watches TV

EXERCISE #2   CASE STUDY OF ABUSE

MATERIALS: Copies of case study for each student

               Paper and pens

               Newsprint and markers or blackboard

PROCEDURE:

1. The instructor should begin by dividing the class
    into subgroups with three to six members. It is
    desirable to have at least three subgroups for
    this activity, so subgroup size should be deter-
    mined accordingly.

2. The instructor explains the activity to students:

        Today we are going to examine a hypothetical
        case study which centers on an abusing family.
        Each of you will receive a copy of the vital
        information in this case. Once you have
        familiarized yourself with the particulars of
        the case, you will be asked to work together
        as a group to develop a "PIP" or Preliminary
        Intervention Plan. Your plan should include
        the following information:

    a. Identification of specific problems in the
        family system.

    b. Recommendations for specific intervention
        strategies which could be used with this
        family.

    c. A detailed description of the social worker's
        tasks.

    d. Comprehensive list of outside agency referrals
        which might be used for this family.

    NOTE: Key words which are underlined should be
        listed on a newsprint or blackboard. You will
        have about fifteen minutes to work on this
        task. Each group will then be asked to pre-
        sent its "PIP" to the class.

3. Hand out student copies of the case study. Allow
    fifteen to twenty minutes for group work. When

time has elapsed, reconvene small groups for full class discussion.

PROCESSING:

1. Ask one member from each subgroup to report the information from the group's Preliminary Intervention Plan. If you are working with a large class, a full report may be too time-consuming. If so, focus on information from Section B. It would be advisable to develop a composite list of specific suggestions on newsprints or on the blackboard.

2. Some possible questions for discussion:

    a. Which parts of this task were easiest for you? Why?

    b. Which parts of this task were more difficult for you? Why?

    c. Were there any strong differences of opinion among your group members? If so, please explain.

    d. Do you think that most social service agencies would follow your "PIP"? Why?

    e. Do you think this case calls for criminal prosecution? Do you think most agencies would attempt prosecution?

    f. How do you think you might feel if you were assigned to interview this mother?

    g. What have you learned from this activity?

    If the instructor used the Case Study of Neglect from Chapter IV, the following questions might also be used:

    a. What similarities did you find in examining this case and the previous case of neglect?

    b. What differences did you find?

    c. In general, which case appears to present the greater challenge to the social worker?

d. If you could choose, which case would you prefer to tackle? Why.

CASE STUDY OF ABUSE

This case involves a family of Hispanic origin.
The four year old female child in the family was
brought to the Emergency Room of a New York City hospital. The young girl received emergency medical treatment for a dislocated shoulder, major bruises, and
shock. Hospital staff recommended that she be admitted for continued observation, but the mother removed
her daughter against medical advice. A check of hospital records showed that the young girl had been
hospitalized twice before with accidental injuries.
The New York City police were notified and an APB was
placed on the mother and the child.

The mother then brought the child to a second hospital in Elizabeth, New Jersey. When the mother was
questioned at the Elizabeth hospital, she identified
the injuries as accidental, stemming from a fall in the
back yard. Her dissatisfaction with the quality of
hospital care in New York was the stated reason for
removing the child against doctor's orders.

The child was admitted to the Elizabeth hospital,
placed under observation, and given further diagnostic
testing. More thorough examination uncovered evidence
of previous bruises and two probable earlier bone frac-
tures. The staff of the pediatric unit were suspicious
of the nature and severity of the injuries. A social
worker from the state protective service agency was
called in for consultation.

The agency social worker who interviewed the mother
had some difficulty understanding her limited English.
She did learn that the mother was a single parent with
just the one daughter. She was receiving public assistance in New York City. When the mother was confronted
with the evidence of previous "accidents" and the con-
cerns of the hospital staff, she became hysterical.
She eventually gave an accurate account of the injuries.

The mother and child had been living with a man in
New York. In this instance and on numerous previous
occasions, the man had beaten the child and the mother.
The mother had moved out of his apartment three times.
However, she had always relented to his remorseful pleas
for forgiveness and returned. After the most recent
beating when she had left to seek medical attention for
her daughter, the boyfriend had threatened their lives

if the mother told the truth about the child's injuries.
The boyfriend owned an illegal handgun.

The mother begged to have the child released from
the hospital immediately. She said that she was currently staying with friends and that she planned to
remain there until she found a job and an apartment in
New Jersey. She claimed that she had not had contact
with the boyfriend since she left his apartment. She
assured the social worker that she did not plan to see
him again. The social worker was suspicious of her
claims.

Preliminary Intervention Plan Guidelines

1.   Identify specific problems in this family system.

2.   Make recommendations for specific interventions
      to be used with this family.

3.   Outline tasks which the social worker would
      perform.

4.   Identify necessary outside agency referrals.

References

Bakan, D., *Slaughter of the Innocents*, San Francisco, CA, Jossey-Bass, 1971.

Chase, N.F., *A Child is Being Beaten*, New York, McGraw Hill, 1976.

Eberling, N.B. (ed), *Child Abuse: Treatment and Intervention*, Acton, Mass., Publishing Sciences Group, Inc., 1975.

Fontana, V., *Somewhere a Child is Crying*, New York, Macmillan Publishing Co., Inc., 1973.

Gelles, R.J., *The Violent Home*, Beverly Hills, CA, Sage Publications, 1972.

Gil, D., *Violence Against Children*, Cambridge, Mass., Harvard University Press, 1970.

Giovananni, J.M., *Defining Child Abuse*, New York, Free Press, 1979.

Helfer, R., *The Battered Child*, Chicago, Ill., University of Chicago Press, 1974.

Helfer, R.E. & Kempe, C.H., *Child Abuse and Neglect - The Family and the Community*, Cambridge, Mass., Ballinger Publishing Co., 1976.

Inglis, R., *Sins of the Fathers*, New York, St. Martins Press, 1978.

Justice, *The Abusing Family*, New York, Human Sciences Press, 1976.

Kempe, C., *Child Abuse and Neglect: The International Journal*, Pergamon Press, 1977.

Kempe, C., *Helping the Battered Child and his Family*, Lippincott, 1972.

Martin, H. (ed), *The Abused Child*, Cambridge, Mass., Ballinger Publishing Co., 1976.

Martin, J.P., *Violence and the Family*, New York, J. Wiley and Sons, Inc., 1978.

Viano, E. (ed), <u>Child Abuse and Neglect - Victimology</u>, An International Journal, Washington, D.C., 1977.

Young, L., <u>Wednesdays Children</u>, New York, McGraw Hill, 1964.

Audio Visual Materials

<u>The Battered Child</u>, Audio Visual Services, The Pennsylvania State University, University Park, PA 16802

<u>Child Abuse: Cradle of Violence</u>, Audio Visual Services, The Pennsylvania State University, University Park, PA 16802

<u>The War of the Eggs</u>, Audio Visual Services, The Pennsylvania State University, University Park, PA 16802

CHAPTER VI

SEXUAL ABUSE

". . . Sexual abuse of children is the last remaining component of the maltreatment syndrome in children that has yet to be faced head on."[1]

"Recognition of sexual molestation in a child is entirely dependent on the individual's inherent willingness to entertain the possibility that the condition may exist."[2]

Sexual abuse is the most under-reported form of child mistreatment. The subject is laden with strong social and cultural taboos. Personal anxiety and ignorance among professionals results in their failure to recognize and treat this problem.

Definitions

Sexual abuse includes any sexual liberties taken by an adult with a child such as intercourse, genital, anal or oral-genital contact, masturbation, fondling, and exposure. There is not always a clear limit between acceptable parental affection and sexual abuse. The criteria for determining whether sexual abuse is occurring is whether or not the parent is attempting to satisfy genital-sexual needs through the child. The primary focus of this chapter will be on incest, defined as sexual activity between members of the same family not married to each other.

Characteristics

Sexual abuse occurs in families where there is a high level of pathology. Family relationships are problematic and intergenerational boundary definitions are blurred. The family is socially isolated. Many sexually abusive parents were sexually abused children. The abuse is often associated with substance abuse.

The actual incidents usually take place within the home. Although the child may be pressured by nature of

[1]S. M. Sgroi, "Sexual Molestation of Children," Children Today, May/June 1975, p. 19.

[2]Ibid., p. 20.

the parental authority, the child is rarely physically forced. The experience is not perceived as all negative. The child often has ambivalent feelings. In a family where sexual abuse is occurring, non-participating family members are usually aware of it and involved by acts of commission or omission.

Most cases of sexual abuse involve the daughter and her father, stepfather or mother's boyfriend. Less frequently there are reported cases between the mother and son, parent and child of the same sex and siblings. The sexual abuse of a child by a stranger poses different problems and will not be discussed in this chapter.

The Family

The literature describes numerous interpretations of the dynamics of a family involved in sexual abuse of the child:

1. The father's hostility and resentment toward his wife is the motive. Through this act, the woman fails as both a wife and a mother.[3]

2. The mother is unable to cope with her responsibilities. She is angry, unhappy and overwhelmed. She is uninterested in a sexual relationship with her husband. The marital situation is generally poor. The mother makes heavy demands on the daughter for child care and homemaking causing her to seem more mature than her years. The daughter becomes the mother's substitute in the adult sexual relationship as well. The mother may encourage this relationship to relieve the pressures she experiences. More often, however, she remains an ineffectual, passive partner, denying the sexual alliance to "keep peace."

3. The father never identified with a positive male role model. He has many unmet emotional needs from childhood; he lacks stability. He presents a strong protective front which proves to be very fragile. He is actually looking for nurturance and affection. When his wife

[3]David R. Walters, Physical and Sexual Abuse of Children - Causes and Treatment, Bloomington, Indiana University Press, 1975.

sees through his strong front and realizes his inability to nurture her, she is disappointed. The result is dissatisfaction and many unmet needs in the marriage. The father turns to his daughter for comfort and a sexual relationship evolves.

A small percentage of sexually abusive parents are psychopathic or psychotic. Some or all of the above characteristics in different combinations may present a truer picture of the abusive family.

The Child in Father-Daughter Incest

There is no stereotypic picture of an abused daughter. Some of the characteristics that may be seen will follow:

The daughter, in fulfilling her part in the role reversal, is the "little mother." She has a poor relationship with her mother, has low self-esteem, and feels unloved and unattractive. She gives in to her father, as this is her only form of affection. She may perceive herself as rescuing her father. She may be very seductive, especially towards her father. The sexual abuse occurs within the context of this relationship.

At puberty, she may wish to end the relationship, but is unable to do so. While she may be reluctant to relinquish the nurturing attention, she now develops a clear sense of the inappropriateness of the behavior. It interferes with the development of peer group relationships. Fear of pregnancy also becomes an issue.

The father is unwilling to end the relationship at this time. The daughter sees reporting the incidents to authorities as more threatening than continuing the relationship. Bringing charges against her father would disrupt any family stability that exists. Her father might go to prison. She might be placed away from home and blamed for her participation. Thus, the adolescent continues the behavior in a state of ambivalence.

Effects of Sexual Abuse

The effects of sexual abuse are varied. The experience may be emotionally damaging as in the inability to have a satisfying adult sexual relationship, but this is not necessarily so. Often the discovery and its aftermath is more traumatic than the experience itself. The damage may come from the reaction of authorities, agency involvement, medical examinations, court testimony, and possible family disruption. The daughter often experiences the most punishment as a result of disclosure. She is often removed from the home, temporarily placed in a shelter, and then moved to a foster home.

Some children do not discuss the problem. Instead, they may act out in other ways. A sudden change in a child's behavior is an indication of a problem. Symptoms such as phobias, hyperactivity, and crying without cause could indicate any number of problems. More specifically, preoccupation with sexual matters, an unusual amount of anxiety about undressing for gym, and fear of being touched are clues that sexual abuse may be occurring.

Intervention

The child is not simply the victim of an adult abuser. Sexual abuse is a manifestation of family pathology. Therefore, a family oriented approach is necessary.

First, the child must be protected. Placement may present a new series of problems and does nothing to change the family dysfunction. Therefore, placement should only be used when the child is in danger, as a temporary measure. A crisis intervention approach with the child is useful because it gives the child a chance to ventilate feelings. The use of dolls in play therapy provides the opportunity for the small child to discuss the experience and any related anxieties.

Intervention with the family should focus on the establishment of appropriate roles and intergenerational boundaries. Work with the couple as a unit can focus on both marital and parental issues. The worker's goal is to enforce society's sanctions without increasing guilt, anxiety and hostility. The approach must be authoritative and direct while being accepting and calm.

In cases of sexual abuse there can be no court support or action without medical backup. A complete medical examination will confirm the abuse and determine whether or not any damage has been done. If the examination is explained and the child is supported through it, it does not need to be a traumatic experience. Medical intervention and reassurance may even be comforting to the child. Without medical corroboration, other interventions may exacerbate the problem rather than help.

Early Identification and Prevention

There are numerous clues that sexual abuse is occurring or is about to occur. In overcrowded conditions, especially when a parent shares a bed with a child of the opposite sex, the situation should be investigated.

An overpossessive and jealous father who restricts his daughter's activities unnaturally may signal potential abuse. Romping play between a father and daughter also warrants suspicion.

Sexual abuse should also be considered in any case where VD is diagnosed in a child. Similarly, a family with a history of sexual abuse of any of its members is high risk for future abuse. In a family with an inadequate mother where the daughter has much of the homemaking and child care responsibilities, the risk of sexual abuse also increases.

When several of these factors exist, the worker must be aware that the situation is ripe for sexual abuse to occur. Intervention may prevent the abuse from occurring. The parents should be encouraged to carry out appropriate parental functions, and should be supported in all areas where they function adequately. Referral to a counseling center for help with marital and family problems is useful. The child should be helped to increase social activities outside of the family. If the abuse is already occurring, then legal and medical steps must be taken in addition to those mentioned above.

FOR STUDY AND DISCUSSION

1. Discuss the major dynamics of families who sexually abuse their children.

2. The feelings of a sexually abused child are often marked by ambivalence. Discuss the reasons for the ambivalence.

3. Describe the clues that sexual abuse is about to occur and discuss methods of prevention.

Student Exercises

These exercises focus on two components of agency intervention in cases of sexual abuse. In Exercise 1, students are given an opportunity to design a model program for servicing abusive families. Exercise 2 presents a case study of sexual abuse which repeats the format developed in the previous two chapters.

EXERCISE #1   DESIGNING A PROGRAM FOR FAMILIES WITH SEXUAL ABUSE

MATERIALS: None

PROCEDURE:

1. The instructor should divide the class into two subgroups of equal membership.

2. Ask members of the first subgroup to move their chairs to form a circle facing inward. Ask members of the second subgroup to form another circle on the perimeter of Group 1, also facing inward.

```
        [2]            [2]
               [1]
        [1]            [1]
  [2]                        [2]
        [1]            [1]

               [1]
        [2]            [2]
```

3. The instructor should explain the activity to the entire group:

> Today we are going to engage in some wishful thinking. Imagine that you are all staff members in a protective service agency. You have been struggling along with myriad problems which always plague such agencies. Then, the unthinkable happens, your director calls you all together for a special staff meeting. She begins the meeting by announcing that an anonymous donor has just contributed $100,000 to your agency.

Your director explains that the donation carries with it specific utilization requirements. Your agency is to design and implement a model program for treating families with episodes of sexual abuse toward children. If the program is successful, the agency will continue to receive $100,000 annually.

It is now your job to initiate the planning process for this program. To do this, Group 1 (inner circle) will begin by focusing on the special problems of families with cases of sexual abuse of children. Once these problems have been discussed, Group 2 (outer circle) will take over to make some preliminary suggestions for program design based on the information from Group 1.

4. Ask members of Group 1 to begin their discussion of the special problems in families with sexually abused children. The group should focus on problems, leaving program planning suggestions to Group 2. Members of Group 2 may not participate in the discussion. They are encouraged to make careful observations of Group 1's discussion. They may find it helpful to take notes. Allow this discussion to continue for ten minutes or until it reaches a natural conclusion.

5. Ask members of Group 1 and Group 2 to change places. Group 2 will become the participating inner circle; Group 1 will become the observing outer circle. Ask members to begin to develop some preliminary recommendations for the design of this $100,000 special program. Encourage group members to incorporate suggestions to cover as many of the problems from Group 1 as possible. Allow this process to continue for ten minutes.

PROCESSING:

1. In a full group discussion, give students from both groups a chance to discuss their reactions to the activity. Your discussion might include the following questions:

   a. Were there any important problem areas which were overlooked in Group 1's discussion?

b. Were there any important program offerings which were overlooked in Group 2's design?

c. How does your preliminary program design compare with existing agency services?

d. What are the most difficult problems confronting any agency which handles cases of sexual abuse?

e. What criteria do you think the agency should use to measure the success of such a program?

f. If this special program were established, would you want to work with the project? Why?

EXERCISE #2   CASE STUDY OF SEXUAL ABUSE

MATERIALS: Copies of case study for each student

Paper and pens

Newsprint and markers or blackboard

1. The instructor should begin by dividing the class into subgroups with three to six members. It is desirable to have at least three subgroups for this activity, so subgroup size should be determined accordingly.

2. The instructor explains the activity to students:

Today we are going to examine a hypothetical case study which centers on an incident of sexual abuse. Each of you will receive a copy of the vital information in this case. Once you have familiarized yourself with the particulars of the case, you will be asked to work together as a group to develop a "PIP" or Preliminary Intervention Plan.

Your plan should include the following information:

a. Identification of <u>specific problems</u> in the family system.

b. Recommendations for <u>specific intervention</u> strategies which could be used with this family.

93

c. A detailed description of the <u>social worker's tasks</u>.

d. Comprehensive lists of outside <u>agency referrals</u> which might be used for this family.

NOTE: Key words which are underlined should be listed on a newsprint or blackboard. You will have about fifteen minutes to work on this task. Each group will then be asked to present its "PIP" to the class.

3. Hand out copies of the case study to students. Allow fifteen to twenty minutes for group discussion. When time has elapsed, reconvene small groups for full class discussion.

PROCESSING:

1. Ask one member from each subgroup to report the information from the group's Preliminary Intervention Plan. If you are working with a large class, a full report may be too time consuming. If so, focus on information from Section B. It would be advisable to develop a composite list of specific suggestions on newsprints or on the blackboard.

2. Some possible questions for discussion:

a. Which part of this task was easiest for you? Why?

b. Which part of this task was most difficult for you? Why?

c. How do you think you would feel if you were assigned to this case?

d. Which family member(s) would you be most comfortable working with? Most uncomfortable? Why?

e. What legal action would you recommend in this case?

f. What special skills would you need to develop to work with this family?

g. What have you learned from this activity?

3. If the case studies in Chapter IV and Chapter V were discussed, your questions might include the following:

   a. How does this case compare to those which you examined in Chapter IV and/or Chapter V?

   b. In which of the cases do you see the greatest likelihood of successful intervention? Why?

   c. If you could choose to work with just one of these families, which family would you select? Why?

   d. What do you see as the greatest challenge involved in working with neglecting and abusive families?

CASE STUDY OF SEXUAL ABUSE

This case was initiated when a fifteen year old girl walked into a local police station to charge her father with the crime of sexual abuse.

The girl is the second of six children in a middle-class family. She has three brothers, age seventeen, thirteen and four. She also has two sisters, age nine and seven. Her father had worked as a supervisor in an auto plant until three months ago when he was layed off because of a plant closing. Her mother is a full-time homemaker with no work experience outside the home.

In an interview with a case worker from the state protective service agency, the girl explained that her father's abusive behavior had begun when she was ten years old. His initial activities included genital exposure and fondling. Once she had reached puberty, he began to demand that she participate in intercourse with him. She described her father as controlling and extremely moody. She reported that his advances had been episodic until recently, when his joblessness and subsequent frustration had caused him to become more aggressive and demanding.

When the girl was asked if her mother knew about the father's abusive behavior, she said that she wasn't sure. She believed that her mother did know but chose to overlook the problem. The girl described her mother as meek and ineffectual. She said that her mother always complained about her family responsibilities. In response to these complaints, the girl had taken on many of the housekeeping chores. She also fulfilled many of the child care needs for her younger brothers and sisters.

The case worker asked about the girl's decision to press charges against her father. The girl's response was vague and defensive. She said that she was afraid that her father would also abuse her two younger sisters, who were approaching the age at which he had begun to abuse her. She refused to discuss any of her personal feelings about her experiences.

At the present time, the girl is living at the home of a friend. She has been totally ostracized by her family. Her attendance at school has become sporadic. She has withdrawm from her friends. Her relationship with her host family has deteriorated as she shows progressive signs of severe depression.

The preliminary hearing for her case has been cancelled three times. No further court date has been scheduled.

Preliminary Intervention Plan Guidelines

1. Identify specific problems in this family system.

2. Make recommendations for specific interventions to be used with this family.

3. Outline tasks which social worker would perform.

4. Identify necessary outside agency referrals.

References

Brant, R.S., Tisza, V.B., "The Sexually Misused Child," American Journal of Orthopsychiatry, 47 (1) January 1977, pp. 80-90.

De Courcy, P., The Silent Tragedy, Port Washington, NY, Alfred Publishing Co., 1973.

De Francis, V., "Protecting the Child Victim of Sex Crimes Committed by Adults," Denver, Colorado, Children's Division, American Humane Assoc., 1969.

Finkelhor, D., Sexually Victimized Children, NY, Free Press, 1979.

Geiser, R.L., Hidden Victim: Sexual Abuse of the Child, Boston, Mass., Beacon Press, 1979.

Justice, B., The Broken Taboo, Human Sciences Press, 1979.

Rosenfeld, "Incest and Sexual Abuse of Children," Journal of the American Assoc. of Child Psychiatry, 16, 1977, pp. 334-336.

Schultz, et. al., "The Child Sex Victim: Social, Psychological and Legal Perspectives," Child Welfare, 52, March 1973, pp. 147-148.

Waters, D.R., Physical and Sexual Abuse of Children, Bloomington, Ind., University Press, 1975.

Audio Visual Materials

Childhood Sexual Abuse, Audio Visual Services, The Pennsylvania State University, University Park, PA 16802

Incest: The Victim Nobody Believes, MTI Teleprograms, Inc., 4825 N. Scott Street, Schiller Park, Ill. 60176.

Incest: Who & Why, School of Social Work, The University of Wisconsin, 425 Henry Mall, Madison, Wis. 53706

CHAPTER VII

SUPPORTIVE SERVICES

Supportive services represent the first line of defense in working with abusive and neglecting parents. All interventions are external to the family structure. The parents remain in charge of the household. The children remain in their own home. Success is based on the parents' motivation and capacity for change.

Supportive services primarily exist in the form of counseling centers. Community Mental Health Centers, Family Service Agencies, Child Guidance Clinics, and private mental health practitioners all provide supportive services. The initial involvement of protective service agencies is often in the form of counseling and supportive services to troubled families. The services provided by these sources vary in form.

Individual intervention is used to provide a relationship which supports, models, teaches, and provides insights in a growth promoting context. This "corrective" experience enables the parent to change personally and, in turn, function as a more responsible parent.

When the problem exists in the child or the parent-child interaction, a family approach is often used. The assumption is that a faulty interaction within the family causes, or exacerbates, the problem. Help is based on correcting this faulty interaction.

Group intervention is based on the assumption that reducing social isolation and improving interpersonal functioning will enable the parent to fulfill more effectively the parental role.

Family Life Education programs exist on the assumption that many problems are based on lack of knowledge and experience. Providing this knowledge may correct some existing problems and prevent many others.

Self-help groups provide an option for those who need help but do not get it because they will not see a professional. The fact that the other group members have the same problem provides the atmosphere which enables the parent to admit the problem and use the help offered.

Supportive services are voluntary in nature. Many people who need help do not apply for service. Many who apply do not follow through. The client population is often hostile toward the helping professionals. This hostility creates barriers which prevent voluntary services from being effective. Therefore, supportive services have limited effectiveness in Child Welfare programs.

Parents Anonymous

Parents Anonymous is a self-help organization founded in 1971. Its thrust is to reduce and prevent child abuse within the family. It is a teaching and therapeutic group service operated for and by the consumer. The group offers problem focused help in a non-judgmental atmosphere. They provide a safe, secure place to go meet where others have the same problem and talk about feelings without the fear of being judged or put down. The emphasis is on giving the parent alternate behaviors in times of stress instead of abusing the child. The organization is based on a child rearing model emphasizing self-sacrifice, nonviolence, non-directive love, unconditional positive regard, guidance and support. Parents Anonymous is a militantly anti-abuse organization. Although they make extensive efforts to help their members, they will report a member to authorities if they feel that it is necessary.

Underlying Assumptions

Parents Anonymous defines abuse as an outward manifestation of the abuser's problem, rather than the problem itself. Therefore, their emphasis is on helping the parent to meet needs and solve problems. A member must admit to being a child abuser and express a desire to change before the individual can be helped. Accountability to the group is an important factor contributing to the members' ability to develop self-control. The organization values the concepts of confidentiality and anonymity. They, therefore, encourage people to use first names only.

Parents Anonymous is an option for those who need help, but are reluctant to seek it because they are fearful of professionals. The self-help concept, with others having the same problems, in a setting that respects confidentiality, all contribute to the attractiveness of this organization.

Organizational Structure

The organization is based on the Alcoholics Anonymous model. Since its inception in 1971, over 800 chapters have been formed throughout the country. Each chapter has a chairperson and a sponsor. The chairperson is the guiding force of the chapter. The chairperson serves as the leader of the meeting. The chairperson has or had a child abuse problem. This leader is chosen by the group members and serves a term of indefinite duration.

The sponsor is a professional, who volunteers time to the group. The sponsor's primary responsibilities include helping the chairperson to be a strong, effective leader and serving as a backup resource person. The sponsor may train the chairperson in some cases and is available to answer questions when needed. The sponsor serves as a key person for those needing additional services by making referrals and helping to bridge the gap between the person and the professional service. The sponsor remains as a background figure and does not run the meetings.

The meetings are scheduled for two hours per week, in a safe, neutral place. The Red Cross, YMCA or church facility is often used rather than the mental health or protective service office.

The focus of the meeting is to discuss how to deal more effectively with here-and-now problems of child rearing. Concrete, specific help is offered. No pressure is placed on members to "confess" or tell their stories, but the supportive atmosphere enables people to share their feelings and experiences. Parents Anonymous encourages personal involvement between members. The members exchange phone numbers so that everyone has someone to call at a time of crisis. At their first meeting, new members receive a handbook entitled, "I am a Parents Anonymous Parent," a handbook which is used nationwide and presents the philosophy of the organization.

Program Goals

The goal of Parents Anonymous is to reduce and prevent child mistreatment. This is done by reducing the social isolation of the parents through a support system. The meeting provides time away from the family,

offering fun, friendship, and a place to talk about personal problems. The members can help each other to
develop an understanding of their problems and share
positive behavioral alternatives. This positive and
supportive group experience can help parents to feel
better about themselves. This, in turn, helps parents
to feel good about family members.

Men and women come to Parents Anonymous through a
variety of sources. Most members are voluntary self-
referrals. They hear of the organization through
friends or mass media publicity. Social agencies and
police departments make referrals when they feel it is
appropriate. The courts have begun to mandate attendance at meetings for abusing parents as a condition
of probation.

"Parents Anonymous Frontiers" is the organization's
monthly newsletter. This is published both to keep its
members informed and to educate professionals to the
workings of the organization.

FOR STUDY AND DISCUSSION

1.   Discuss some of the conditions that would indicate
     that supportive services would be sufficient to
     help the family.

2.   Discuss some of the ways in which Family Life
     Education programs can contribute to improved
     family functioning.

3.   Discuss some of the ways in which Parents Anonymous
     reduces the problem of child maltreatment.

Student Exercises

These exercises serve two distinct purposes. In Exercise 1, students are asked to role play a session in a family life education group. Exercise 2 offers a self-assessment inventory designed to help students evaluate their personal strengths and weaknesses as future social workers.

EXERCISE #1   ROLE PLAY: FAMILY LIFE EDUCATION GROUP

MATERIALS: Role descriptions for each of the role play participants

PROCEDURE:

1. The instructor begins by explaining the activity to the class:

> As future child welfare workers, you may be called upon to lead a family life education group. As the leader of such a group, you will be expected to facilitate the group process by providing a sense of direction, moderating group discussions, and mediating group conflicts if they arise. To give you an experience of what that might be like, we are now going to role play a simulated family life education group for parents.

2. The instructor asks for ten volunteers to participate in the role play.

3. The instructor sets the scene and makes role assignments:

a. Our family life education group has been meeting for several weeks. The group has ten members; two co-leaders and eight parents. The focus for this session is family time activities.

b. To participants: I will now give each of you a slip of paper describing your role. Please take a minute and think about your character. The two co-leaders may want to decide on a procedure for opening the meeting. Hand out role descriptions to participants.

103

c. To observers: Those of you who are not active-
ly participating in this activity will serve
as observers. As the role play progresses,
please jot down your observations, focusing
on the strengths and weaknesses of the group
process. You may also want to jot down your
suggestions for possible improvements.

d. Allow two minutes for participants to familiar-
ize themselves with their roles. Have participants form a circle with observers outside the
group.

4. Carry out the role play. Allow about fifteen
minutes for this part of the exercise. When the
time is up, ask participants to stop the exercise
and return to full group discussion.

PROCESSING:

1. In a full group discussion, ask class members to
comment on their experiences.

2. Your discussion might cover the following questions:

a. To Parents

1) How did it feel to be a part of this group?
2) What did you learn about parental behavior?
3) What did you like about the group experience?
4) What did you dislike?

b. To Co-Leaders

1) How did you feel as a co-leader in the
group?
2) What did you learn about group leadership?
3) What did you enjoy most about your role?
4) What did you dislike about your role?
5) Would you like to lead this type of group?

c. To Observers

1) What did you observe in this group which
impressed you?
2) What specific behaviors were most helpful?
3) What trouble spots did you identify?

4) What changes would you recommend to improve this group's experience?

d. <u>General</u>

1) What do you see as the potential value of this form of supportive services?
2) What do you see as the hazards in running this type of group?
3) What skills are necessary for effective group leadership?
4) What did you learn from this activity?

Role Descriptions

1. Co-Leader

   You are an agency worker, serving as a co-leader of this group. The topic for this meeting is family enrichment activities. You hope to draw upon the resources of the parents to generate a number of activities which families can do to strengthen the family unit. These activities might include family outings, picnics, games, home improvement projects, community service, etc.

2. Co-Leader

   You are an agency worker, serving as a co-leader of this group. The topic for this meeting is family enrichment activities. You hope to draw upon the resources of the parents to generate a number of activities which families can do to strengthen the family unit. These activities might include family outings, picnics, games, home improvement projects, community service, etc.

3. Parent

   You are feeling overwhelmed with your family responsibilities. You want to be a good parent, but you just feel that there's never enough time to do the things that have to be done.

4. Parent

   You have tried organizing family activities in the past and they have never worked. Your children just don't seem to be interested or cooperative.

5. Parent

   You are open to the idea of family activities, but you are sure that your husband or wife will never go along with the idea. You would like to focus on your problems with getting cooperation from your spouse.

6. Parent

   You enrolled in this group to learn how to control your children. You think the whole idea of family life activities is ridiculous. You just want to know how to get your children to do what you want them to do.

7. Parent

   You know a great deal about this topic and you want to make sure that everyone else in the group benefits from your knowledge. If possible, you would like to monopolize the group discussion.

8. Parent

   You are interested and cooperative. The idea of family activities is interesting to you and you are eager to learn as much as you can.

9. Parent

   You are interested and cooperative. The idea of family activities is interesting to you and you are eager to learn as much as you can.

10. Parent

    You are interested and cooperative. The idea of family activities is interesting to you and you are eager to learn as much as you can.

EXERCISE #2   STUDENT SELF-EXPLORATION

MATERIALS: Student self-exploration sheet

              Pencils or pens

PROCEDURE:

1. The instructor begins by explaining the activity
    to students:

    > In any social work setting, one critical
    > factor which influences the quality of the
    > service delivery is the personality of the
    > social worker. Research suggests that there
    > is a positive correlation between the self-
    > esteem level of the social worker and his/
    > her ability to provide effective service to
    > clients.

    > With this in mind, today's activity will give
    > you an opportunity to complete a personal
    > self-concept inventory. By privately assess-
    > ing the degree to which you possess specific
    > personal attributes, you will gain a greater
    > appreciation for your current strengths and
    > you will become more aware of those areas which
    > may need some further development.

2. The instructor should hand out one copy of the
    Student Self-Exploration Sheet to each student.
    Read through the directions at the beginning of
    the exercise. Allow enough time for students to
    complete the exercise without feeling rushed or
    pressured.

3. Once all students have completed their rankings,
    ask each class member to underline the five per-
    sonal attributes on the list which they see as
    most important in the personality of a social
    worker.

4. Ask students to place an asterisk next to the
    five personal attributes which they would like to
    enhance in themselves.

PROCESSING:

1. Divide the class into small groups with no more
    than four students per group. Ask each student
    to take a few minutes to share some thoughts and
    reactions with fellow students. Remind students
    that they do not have to discuss their responses
    to any individual item from the check list if they
    choose to keep them private. Be sure that all stu-

dents have a few minutes to discuss their reactions or responses.

And/Or:

2. Conduct a brief full class discussion. Your discussion questions might include the following:

    a. What characteristics did you identify as most important for a social worker? Why?

    b. What additional characteristics might have been included on your self-exploration list?

    c. In your experience with field placement, how would you evaluate the self-concept of most agency workers?

    d. If the self-concept of the social worker does have a significant effect on his/her job performance, should low self-esteem individuals be screened out of social work programs? Why or why not?

    e. What needs to be done to strengthen the overall self-esteem of social workers?

    f. How do you go about improving your personal attribute ratings?

    g. What have you learned from this activity?

STUDENT SELF-EXPLORATION SHEET

DIRECTIONS: The following is a list of twenty personal attributes which are desirable qualities in a social worker. Please rate yourself on a scale of 0-10 for each of the items on the list (0 = does not possess this characteristic at all; 10 = perfectly developed in this area). NOTE: You may be given an opportunity to discuss your answers with fellow students. You will not be required to discuss any responses which you would prefer to keep private. Please take your time and answer as thoughtfully as possible.

CHARACTERISTIC	RATING (0-10)
A. Self-confident	_____
B. Tactful	_____
C. Emotionally stable	_____
D. Energetic	_____
E. Organized	_____
F. Cooperative	_____
G. Generous	_____
H. Considerate	_____
I. Good-natured	_____
J. Flexible	_____
K. Able to accept criticism	_____
L. Easy to get to know	_____
M. Imaginative	_____
N. Having a sense of humor	_____
O. Friendly	_____
P. Responsible	_____
Q. Ambitious	_____

R.	Open	_____

S.	Trusting of others	_____

T.	Mature	_____

References

Duryea, P., Fontana, R., Alfaro, J., "Child Maltreatment - A New Approach to Educational Programs," Children Today, 7 (5), pp. 13-16, 1978.

Carmody, F.J., Lanier, D., Bradill, D., "Prevention of Child Abuse in Military Families," Children Today, 8 (2), pp. 16-21, 35, 1979.

Collins, M., Child Abuser - A Study of Child Abusers in Self-Help Group Therapy, Littleton, Mass., PSG Publishing Co., 1978.

Polansky, N., "Help for the Helpless," Smith College Studies in Social Work, 49 (3), pp. 169-91, 1979.

Porvell, T.J., "Interpreting Parents Anonymous as a Source of Help for Those with Child Abuse Problems," Child Welfare, 58 (2), pp. 105-114, 1979.

Shorkey, C.T., "A Review of Methods Used in the Treatment of Abusing Parents," Social Casework, 60 (6), pp. 360-367, 1979.

Child Welfare League of America Statement on Social Work Service for Children in Their Own Homes, New York, CWLA, 1977.

Audio Visual Materials

Don't Give Up on Me, Audio Visual Services, The Pennsylvania State University, University Park, PA 16802

CHAPTER VIII

SUPPLEMENTARY SERVICES

"Home life is the highest and finest product of civilization. It is the great moulding force of men and of character. Children should not be deprived of it except for urgent and compelling reasons. . . Except in unusual circumstances, the home should not be broken up for reasons of poverty."[1]

Supplementary services become part of the social system of the family and take over some aspects of the parent role. The family remains intact, with members carrying out all functions that they are able to handle.

Supplementary services include the following:

> Financial Assistance
> Homemaker Service
> Day Care
> Protective Services

Financial Assistance

In our society, it is the parents' responsibility to work and earn the money needed to support the family. When the parents are unable to do this, financial assistance replaces or supplements their income.

Financial assistance programs exist in the form of insurance programs and in Aid to Families with Dependent Children.

Insurance programs include:

> Workmen's Compensation
> Unemployment
> OASDI - Social Security

Workmen's Compensation provides benefits to workers who are injured in an employment related activity.

Unemployment programs are operated by the state, with terms and benefits varying from state to state.

[1]First White House Conference on the Care of Dependent Children, 1910.

Funds are obtained from employer and employee mandatory payroll deductions.

OASDI (Old Age Survivors Disability Insurance) is part of the Social Security Program. It provides benefits to surviving family members of the deceased. Benefits are based on the number of family members and their ages. This program also supports those who are permanently disabled.

AFDC (Aid to Families with Dependent Children) provides support for those who have no resources and are not covered by any insurance program. The program is funded by taxes. AFDC is based on the premise that all people have the right to the basic necessities of life. The family should be maintained as a unit whenever possible.

These income maintenance programs provide cash benefits to those in need. There are, however, major problems with these programs. The benefits are inadequate, especially in these inflationary times. The large bureaucratic network that manages these programs provides conditions ripe for fraud and other abuses.

Homemaker Services

Homemaker services are used when the parent is unavailable or unable to perform adequate child care and homemaking functions. The homemaker takes over any needed responsibilities. Homemaker service is based on the assumption that the best place for the child is in the home. Society has the responsibility to help the parent fulfill the homemaking role. The goal of the homemaker is to strengthen, support, supplement and restore parental functioning to prevent the unnecessary removal of a child from the home.

Homemaker services may be appropriate in various situations. When the parent is absent from the home temporarily as in hospitalization, the homemaker can take over all child care and homemaking responsibilities. When the parent is absent permanently, as in abandonment or death, the homemaker can fill in until permanent arrangements can be made. When the parent is physically present, but the functioning capacity is lowered as in convalescence, the homemaker can function in any capacity that is needed. The homemaker, by serving as a teacher and role model, can also help the

114

parent to develop more adequate skills in child care and homemaking. The homemaker can offer supplemental assistance to the parent who is overwhelmed by the burdens of a difficult situation, such as the care of a sick or handicapped child.

Homemaker services are organized within a social agency. Service is offered to the family with specific goals within the context of an overall agency plan. There are limits to what a homemaker can do. The homemaker is not a R.N. or a maid and should not be expected to serve either function. The goal of the homemaker is to enable the family to reach independence. Therefore, the homemaker does not do anything for the family members that they can do themselves. The homemaker encourages escalating degrees of independent functioning.

The role of the social worker includes training and supervision of the homemaker. The social worker may also be working with the family in formulating the plan in which the homemaker participates.

There are certain potential problems associated with the use of a homemaker. The mother, especially one with a history of difficulty in handling her responsibilities, may feel that her position is being threatened by the homemaker. The children may feel conflicted in responding to someone who acts as a mother, but is not their mother. Having an outsider in the home does represent an intrusion into the privacy of the family. Overall, however, the homemaker's presence requires less of an adjustment than the breakup of the family and the placement of the children in foster care.

Day Care

The purpose of day care is to provide care for the children when their parents are unavailable. It is an organized service for the care of children away from home when circumstances require normal home care to be supplemented.

There are numerous situations when day care services are appropriate. Most children are in day care while their parents work outside of the home. Day care can provide an enriching experience for children. Therapeutic day care can provide the much needed relief to an overwhelmed parent. Day care is useful in a situation where the parent-child relationship is disturbed. For the handicapped child, specialized day care can prevent the need for institutionalization.

Initially, day care usage usually accompanied many serious family and social problems. The social worker had an active role with all families. Today, many people use day care as a normal part of a daily routine and have no need for contact with a social worker.

Social work services are available to help with the family's adjustment to the use of day care. The social worker can identify problems or potential problems and can make appropriate interventions and/or referrals.

The concept of universal day care is a controversial issue. Although it remains as a child welfare priority, universal day care is clearly not a reality in our society today. Prior to the late 1960's, the attitude that a mother of young children should not work prevailed. Therefore, to provide day care was presumably encouraging mothers to work outside the home. Things have changed. For many mothers, employment outside the home is a financial necessity. With the feminist movement came the notion that women should have choices concerning issues that affect their lives. Available high quality day care services are necessary if a woman is to have a real choice as to whether she will work or stay home.

Public interest in day care is growing. Private enterprise has entered into the day care business and is reaping the profits. With the increasing costs of welfare programs, there is interest in getting mothers off welfare and working.

Protective Services

Protective services represent society's interests in child welfare. They can be supportive, supplementary, or substitute. Protective services are specialized social work services to abused, neglected, exploited, or rejected children and their families. The child is the client; the parent is the focus of the service. The philosophy of the service is preventive, non-punitive and rehabilitative. In protective services, the social worker functions in collaboration

with many other professionals. Protective services
carry the judicial power to intervene, with the state
acting as parent to all children. The attempt is made
to ensure the rights of the child without infringing
on the rights of the parents.

The majority of protective service cases involve
child neglect. The process of case finding usually
follows the investigation of a complaint. The initial
assessment is followed by the formulation of a case
plan. The emphasis is placed on maintaining an intact
family. If the parent is concerned and amenable to
receiving help, this argues against removal and placement of the child. The parents do not have the right
to refuse service. The agency remains involved with
the family until the danger to the child is eliminated.

The intervention plan may involve casework services, supplementary services, or voluntary foster
placement. As a last resort, with uncooperative families, the agency may take court action to remove the
child from the home. The social worker, in making the
initial contact, must make a clear, direct and frank
statement of purpose. The worker attempts to enlist
the aid of the parents in determining what is happening.
Voluntary usage of the service is encouraged. The
parents, feeling threatened, may react with hostility.
The worker should respond with support and understanding, treating them as troubled, needy people.

When the child is in eminent danger and the parents
refuse help, court action becomes necessary. This is
for the protection of the child, not punishment of the
parents. Legal action is often a mobilizing and moti-
vating force. Only a small minority of cases (less
than 10%) actually involve court action. Use of legal
action clearly changes the worker's role from helper
to adversary. The court is equally concerned with protecting the rights of the parents as well as in the
protection of the child. The burden of proof is with
the social worker to make a case that will stand up in
court. The court can rule to place the child in temporary foster care or to terminate parental rights.
Conditions for this vary from state to state.

FOR STUDY AND DISCUSSION

1. Discuss some of the ways in which supplementary
    services can prevent the need for placement of
    a child.

117

2. The idea of universal day care remains as a controversial issue. Discuss some of the factors surrounding this controversy.

3. The protective service worker may be seen as a helper or an adversary. Discuss the aspects of this role which contribute to this dual perception.

Student Exercises

These exercises serve two distinct purposes. Exercise 1 asks students to assume the roles of political lobbyists who are attempting to influence legislation on supplemental services. Exercise 2 encourages students to further explore the personal values which they bring to their future careers in social work.

EXERCISE #1   SOCIAL WORK POLICY LOBBY

MATERIALS: Paper and pens or pencils

Blackboard/chalk or newsprint and markers

PROCEDURE:

1. The instructor begins by explaining the activity to the class:

> In today's class, we have focused on the area of supplemental services. We have looked at those services which are currently available and touched upon additional services which would be desirable. In order to procure these desirable services, it will be necessary for workers in the field to convince legislators of the need for expanded services. This advocacy function may be an important element of your role as a future social worker. Today, you will have an opportunity to try your hand at lobbying for a specific element of supplemental services.

2. Divide the class into three groups. Give specific instructions for the activity:

> You are all working for government agencies. You have just been told that your group will serve as a special task force. Each group will focus on one specific area of potential supplemental services.
>
> Group 1 - Universal Day Care
> Group 2 - Expanded Homemaker Services
> Group 3 - Guaranteed Minimal Family Income
>
> Your task force will be called upon to present its recommendations to the Program Development

119

Committee of the Department of Health and Human Services. This committee will determine future appropriations based on the strength of your presentation.

a. Demonstration of need
b. Recommendations for program implementation
c. Potential benefits of this program
d. Defense of monetary expenditures

You will have about twenty minutes to develop your preliminary recommendations.

NOTE: These categories should be listed on a blackboard or newsprint.

3. Allow approximately twenty to thirty minutes for groups to develop their presentations. At the end of this time, reconvene for full group discussion.

PROCESSING:

1. Ask one representative from each group to present a summary of the group's recommendations.

2. Conduct a summary discussion. Your discussion might include the following questions:

a. Of the three supplemental service areas, which area do you see as most important? Why?

b. Based on the reports which you have just heard, which program would have the best chance of receiving funding? Why?

c. Do you think you would enjoy doing this type of social service advocacy work? Why or why not?

d. What special skills would you need to develop to function in this role?

e. What have you learned by participating in this activity?

EXERCISE #2   THE MIRACLE WORKERS

MATERIALS: "Miracle Worker" activity sheet for each
              student

              Pens or pencils

              Newsprint and marker or blackboard and
              chalk

PROCEDURE:

1. The instructor begins by explaining the activity
    to the class:

        Today we are going to be introduced to some
        very unique people. They are known as the
        "Miracle Workers." Each "Miracle Worker"
        represents a personal value which may be im-
        portant to you and/or your future clients.
        As we take part in this activity, we will
        identify those "Miracle Workers" who are most
        attractive to us and those who might be most
        attractive to our clients.

2. Hand out the "Miracle Worker" activity sheet to
    each student. Go over the directions. If time
    permits, you may choose to read through the list
    of "Miracle Workers" with the class. Allow enough
    time for students to write out their responses to
    the exercise.

PROCESSING:

1. Ask students to form discussion groups with three
    or four members. On a newsprint or on the black-
    board, post the following questions for discussion:

    a. Which "Miracle Workers" were most attractive
        to you?

    b. Why do you think you valued these "Miracle
        Workers" over others on the list?

    c. How would you expect your lists to compare or
        contrast with lists which your future clients
        might make?

    d. What are some factors which might contribute

to differences in these lists?

Allow about fifteen minutes for small group discussion.

2. Close with a full group discussion. Ask class members to share their responses focusing on the last two questions.

THE MIRACLE WORKERS

DIRECTIONS: A group of ten experts, considered miracle workers by those who have used their
services, have agreed to provide these
services for the members of this class.
Their extraordinary skills are guaran-
teed to be 100% effective. It is up to
you to decide which of these people can
best provide you with what you want.
Rank order the following miracle workers
in relation to their attractiveness to
you; #1 should be most attractive, #10
should be least attractive.

_____   a.   Dr. Redo is a noted plastic surgeon. He
can make you look exactly as you want to
look by means of a new painless technique. He also uses harmless hormones to
alter body structures and size. Your
ideal physical appearance can be a
reality.

_____   b.   Ms. Gotta Job is a job placement expert.
The job of your choice in the location
of your choice will always be yours.

_____   c.   Jedediah Methuselah guarantees you long
life to the age of 200 with your aging
process slowed down proportionately. At
age 60, you will look and feel like 20.

_____   d.   Dr. Masters Johnson is an expert in the
area of sexual relations. He guarantees
that you will be the perfect male or
female, will enjoy sex, and will bring
pleasure to others.

_____   e.   Dr. Yin Yang is a holistic health expert.
He will provide you with perfect health
and protection from physical injury
throughout your life.

_____   f.   "Pop" Larity guarantees that you will
have all the friends you want now and in
the future. You will find it easy to
approach those you like and they will
find you easily approachable.

_____ g. Dr. Charlotte Smart will develop your common sense and your intelligence to the level of a genius. You will remain at this level through your entire lifetime.

_____ h. Rocky Fellah guarantees that wealth will be yours with schemes for earning millions within weeks.

_____ i. Dr. Claire Voyant answers all your questions about the future with her soothsayer talents.

_____ j. Dr. Noya Self guarantees that you will have self-knowledge, self-liking, self-respect, and self-confidence. True self-assurance will be yours.

Adapted from Values Clarification: A Handbook of Practical Strategies For Teachers and Students. Simon, Howe, and Kirschenbaum, New York: Hart Publishing Co., 1972.

References

Duryea, P., Fontana, W., Alfara, J., "Child Maltreatment - A New Approach to Education Programs," <u>Children Today</u>, 7 (5), pp. 13-16, 1978.

Carmody, F.J., Lanier, D., Bardill, D., "Prevention of Child Abuse in Military Families," <u>Children Today</u>, 8 (2) pp. 16-21-23, 35, 1979.

Flanzraich, Dunsavage, "Role Reversal in Abused/Neglected Families: Implications for Child Welfare Workers," <u>Children Today</u>, 6 (6), pp. 13-15, 36, 1977.

Le Blang, T.R., "The Family Stress Consultation Team: An Illinois Approach to Protective Services," <u>Child Welfare</u>, 58 (7), pp. 597-604, 1979.

Polansky, N., "Help for the Helpless," <u>Smith College Studies in Social Work</u>, 49 (3), pp. 169-91, 1979.

Shorkey, C.T., "A Review of Methods Used in the Treatment of Abusing Parents," <u>Social Casework</u>, 60 (6), pp. 360-67, 1979.

<u>Child Welfare League of America Statement on Social Work Service for Children in Their Own Homes</u>, New York, CWLA, 1977.

Audio Visual Materials

<u>Day Care Today</u>, Audio Visual Services, The Pennsylvania State University, University Park, PA 16802.

<u>Operation Head Start</u>, Audio Visual Services, The Pennsylvania State University, University Park, PA 16802.

CHAPTER IX

HOME BASED CARE

Home based care refers to an approach to family support and assistance which focuses on services which can be obtained in or near the family home. These services may exist within the pre-existing socially sanctioned institutions such as the health, educational, legal, welfare and industrial systems. They may include the informal supports that exist with family, friends, neighbors, and volunteers. The services also include those developed to meet any special needs of a particular family.

Traditionally, the concept of home based care has been applied to homemakers and visiting nurses who enter a home to serve specific family needs. Currently, home based care is being used to describe a much broader range of services. The family is viewed as a system within the community and the plan is to meet the total needs of this system. Although homemaker or visiting nurse services may be included in a family plan, home based care frequently involves much more.

Historical Development of Home Based Services

Home based care represents a change in the philosophy and manner of delivery of child welfare services. The concept has been developed within the past ten years. The United States has historically emphasized the use of institutions to deal with social problems. Although there has been much evidence that institutions may have detrimental effects on those they serve, they have continued to be used for large numbers of people.[1]

The initial movement away from the use of institutions for child welfare problems led to the use of foster family homes. The child was still separated from the family. There were a number of reasons for this. Child welfare workers have tended to over identify with children and have felt the need to "rescue" them. They underestimated the ability of the family to change. They lacked the skills and resources to enable them to do anything else.

[1]Marvin Bryce, et. al., Treating Families in the Home, Springfield, Illinois: Charles C. Thomas, 1981. p.6.

The Child Welfare League of America has always maintained a policy that emphasized keeping the family together. Throughout the twentieth century, the United States has paid lip service to the value of keeping the child in the home with the family. Yet, the most well developed child welfare services are those that involve placement. Until the 1980 legislation, most child welfare financial assistance was earmarked for substitute care.

With the Adoption Assistance and Child Welfare Act of 1980, came a shift in emphasis. Funding is now available for preventive programs. Home based problems are also eligible for funding. In order to receive funding for substitute care, a demonstration of attempts to prevent placement must be made. The major thrust of this act is toward the creation of a permanent plan for the child, with continuity within the biological family given priority.

Underlying Assumptions

In the United States, the family is the primary social institution. There is a commitment to maintaining the family as a unit since it seems that it cannot be adequately replaced. Home based care provides assistance to the family in a way that does not bypass or replace the parents.

There is growing evidence that foster home care and institutionalization have not worked for large numbers of people. The separation of a young child from the family often has a detrimental effect on the child's development.[2] Home based care provides an alternative to substitute care for many families.

Home based care offers many economic advantages. Substitute care is very expensive. In this country, the length of substitute care placements averages three years.[3] Once a child is removed from the home, other family members usually receive additional services. There may even be further placements of other

[2]Ibid.

[3]"Home Based Family Centered Service: A View from the Child Welfare Sector," National Clearinghouse for Home Based Services to Children and Their Families, Oakdale, Iowa: The University of Iowa, p. 5.

128

children in the family. Home based care, with its emphasis on family preservation, offers a viable, cost effective alternative to substitute care.

Characteristics of Home Based Care

In home based care, the first and greatest resource investment is to the child and family in the interest of maintaining and strengthening the family and avoiding placement. The services are complete, comprehensive, and intense. They are individualized and personal. The importance of relationship is valued. Services are available twenty-four hours a day, every day of the year. The service setting is primarily the home, but includes the family's ecological system (those outside organizations with which the family interacts). The parents remain in charge as primary caretakers. They are expected to take an active role in the development and implementation of a family plan. Families are encouraged to make maximum use of existing family resources. When gaps or weaknesses in the family system exist, home based care workers can provide direct service to the family. This service may take the form of direct intervention, referral to the appropriate community service agency, or if no appropriate service agency exists, the creation of new services.

The Role of the Social Worker

Home based care programs have an eclectic orientation. They are staffed by bachelor level professionals who work in teams. They work with a family for an average of seven months.

Once an in-home evaluation is done, a work schedule is developed that is deemed appropriate to meet the family's needs. In recruiting staff, home based care programs emphasize low staff turnover to enable one team to complete its work with a family. The workers have small, manageable case loads. The services continue as long as necessary.

Uses of Home Based Care

Home based care services were designed to decrease the number of children who must go into substitute care. The pilot projects have shown impressive results in their ability to do this.[4] These services are also use-

[4]Ibid.

ful in preventing child abuse and neglect in high risk families.

Home based care can be used in conjunction with substitute care placement. A child may be placed in substitute care while the home base care team continues to work with the family, thus minimizing the time of family separation. When the child is returned to the home, home based care services can aid in the transition, helping to bridge the gap between the two homes. Home based services increase the chances of the child successfully returning home.

Services Provided

Many pilot projects have sprouted up throughout the country in the last decade. Although each program has its own unique features and they all differ in the services provided and manner of delivery, there are some common features to most home based care programs. Most programs provide twenty-four hour emergency services. For unsupervised children, the programs will provide caretakers in the home until permanent arrangements can be made. Parent-aides, homemakers, and visiting nurses also deliver services in home based programs. Since the goal of the program is to enable the family to function without services, the programs provide in-home parent education through both teaching and role modeling.

The Future of Home Based Care

It would appear that much of the future of child welfare would include home based services. Home based care services provide a method of complying with the requirements of the 1980 legislation. These programs have been able to prevent placement in 70% of the cases.[5] If these services are to be widely used, judges and social workers must be made aware of their value. Professionals must be trained and willing to work the long, intensive hours. Programs must be assured adequate and continual funding.

[5]Ibid.

FOR STUDY AND DISCUSSION

1. The ideas represented in home based care are not new. The approach appears to be sound. Discuss some of the reasons why you feel that home based services are not more widespread.

2. Discuss the ways in which home based services can enable a state to comply with the Federal Regulations set out in the Adoption Assistance and Child Welfare Act of 1980.

3. Devise a home based service plan for one of the families that you are presently working with.

Student Exercises

These exercises serve two distinct purposes. In Exercise 1 students are asked to evaluate the strengths and weaknesses of home based care programs from the vantage point of the family and the social worker. Exercise 2 asks students to explore possible trends in child welfare service delivery in the next two decades.

EXERCISE #1   PROS AND CONS OF HOME BASED CARE

MATERIALS: Paper, pens or pencils

PROCEDURE:

1.   The instructor begins by giving a brief intro-
     duction to the activity:

          As we have discussed in class, the concept
          of home based care is a relatively new
          approach to family service. As such, it is
          still in the evaluative stage of development.
          As future social workers who may have an
          opportunity to work as home based care
          workers, it may be helpful for us to examine
          some of the pros and cons of this mode of
          intervention as it affects the client family
          and the social worker.

2.   Divide the class into two groups. Explain the
     task to both groups:

          Group 1: For the purpose of this exercise, you
          will assume the role of the family in need of
          social service agency assistance. You have
          been offered the services of a home based care
          team. From your vantage point, what would be
          the advantages and disadvantages of becoming
          involved in this process? As a group, please
          make a list explaining the pros and cons of
          home based care services.

          Group II: For the purpose of this exercise,
          you will assume the role of social workers
          who are being given an opportunity to join a
          home based care team. From your vantage point,
          what are the advantages and disadvantages of
          this position. As a group, please make a list

132

explaining the pros and cons of serving as a home based care worker.

3. Allow about fifteen minutes for group discussion.

PROCESSING:

1. Return to full class focus. Ask each group to report on the results of their discussion. It may be helpful to develop a composite list of major points.

2. Conduct a general discussion drawing on the information presented by the groups. Discussion questions might include the following:

    a. What factors might influence a family's willingness to become involved in a home based care program?

    b. Do you think that family roles (father, mother, child) would have any influence on willingness or reluctance to become involved in a home based care program?

    c. As a social worker, what personal factors might influence your willingness to become a home based care worker?

    d. What special skills would you need to function as a home based care worker?

    e. Based on our discussion, do you think you would be interested in joining a home based care team?

    f. Do you believe that home based care will become a predominant method of intervention in the future? Why or why not?

    g. What did you learn from this activity?

EXERCISE #2:   THINKING AHEAD: CHILD WELFARE IN THE
                YEAR 2000

MATERIALS: The Year 2000: Stimulus Questions Sheet

PROCEDURE:

1. The instructor begins by explaining the activity
    to students:

>   As future practitioners in the social work
>   field, most of your energies will be directed
>   toward the overwhelming number of daily pro-
>   blems which will be brought to your agencies.
>   However, as we attempt to improve the existing
>   conditions for children in need, it is also
>   important for us to look to the future to be
>   prepared for the demands which will be put
>   upon us in years to come. In a sense, we must
>   try to be social work visionaries, predicting
>   the future direction of our society and anti-
>   cipating the needs of our children. Today,
>   we're going to try our hand at predicting the
>   future.

2. Divide the class into small groups of four to six
    members. Hand out a list of stimulus questions
    to each student and give specific instructions:

>   The sheet which you have just received is
>   designed to get you thinking about the possible
>   trends in child welfare during the next two
>   decades. Please read through the list pri-
>   vately and then conduct an informal discussion
>   sharing your thoughts and predictions about
>   the future of our society. You will have
>   about twenty minutes to discuss your ideas.

PROCESSING:

1. Return to full class discussion. Ask one member
    of each group to give a brief summarization of
    the major ideas generated in the small group
    discussion.

2. Drawing on the information reported by small
    groups, ask students to consider future directions
    in child welfare services. Your discussion might
    include the following questions:

134

a. What do you see as future directions in child welfare work?

b. Which problem areas will receive the most attention in the future?

c. Do you predict any major changes in the current service delivery systems?

d. What changes do you see in the role of the child welfare worker?

e. What changes will be made in the training procedures for child welfare workers?

f. Do you see yourself working in the field of child welfare in the year 2000? If yes, what would you be doing? Would you be happy with your job?

THE YEAR 2000: STIMULUS QUESTIONS

1. Will the United States exist in the same basic structure that it exists today?

2. Will we still have a strong federal government determining the direction of our social service policy?

3. Will there be major changes in the demographic makeup of our country?

4. What will the economic climate be like?

5. What will be the most difficult problems facing our society?

6. Will "the family" as we know it today still exist?

7. What will the "average family" look like?

8. What changes will occur in parenting roles and responsibilities?

9. How will the children compare with the children of today?

10. What will be the most difficult problems affecting children?

References

Bryce, M., "Home Based Family Centered Care: Problems and Perspectives," Treating Families In The Home, Springfield, Illinois, Chas. C. Thomas, 1981.

Bryce, M., "Home Based Care: Development & Rationale," Home Based Services for Children and Families, Springfield, Illinois, Chas. C. Thomas, 1979.

Bryce, M. & Maybanks, S. eds., "Policy, Practice & Research," Home Based Services for Children and Families, Springfield, Illinois, Chas. C. Thomas, 1979.

Bryce, M. & Lloyd, J. eds., "An Alternative to Placement," Treating Families in the Home, Springfield, Illinois, Chas. C. Thomas, 1981.

Burt, M., "Final Results of the Nashville Comprehensive Emergency Services Project," Child Welfare, 55 (9), November 1976, pp. 661-664.

Goldstein, H., "Providing Services to Children in Their Own Homes: An Approach That Can Reduce Foster Placement," Children Today 2 (4), July/August 1973, pp. 2-7.

Hirsh, J. & Gailey, J., et. al., "A Child Welfare Agency's Program of Service to Children in Their Own Homes," Child Welfare 55 (3), March 1976, pp. 193-204.

Jones, Mary A., "Reducing Foster Care Through Services to Families," Children Today 5 (6), November/December 1976, pp. 6-10.

Jones, M., A Second Chance for Families: Evaluation of a Program to Reduce Foster Care, New York, Child Welfare League of America, 1976.

Karlshruber, A., "The Non Professional as a Psychotherapeutic Agent," American Journal of Community Psychology 2 (1), March 1974, pp. 61-77.

Kempe, C. & Helfer, R., "Innovative Therapeutic Approaches," Helping the Battered Child and His Family, Philadelphia, PA. 45 (2), 1977, pp. 667-673.

Meier, E., "Focused Treatment for Children at Home," Children, 9 (1), January/February 1962, pp. 15-20.

Shyne, A., et. al., "Filling a Gap in Child Welfare Research: Service to Children in Their Own Homes," Child Welfare 51 (9), November 1972, pp. 562-573.

Speck, R., "Family Therapy in the Home," Journal of Marriage and the Family 26 (1), February 1964, pp. 72-76.

Turitz, Aitha R., "Obstacles to Services for Children in Their Own Homes," Child Welfare 40 (6), June 1961, pp. 1-6, 27.

Tuszynski, Ann & David J., "An Alternative Approach to the Treatment of Protective Service Families," Social Casework 59 (3), March 1978, pp. 175-179.

Audio Visual Materials

Home and Community Treatment: Activating Family Change, Mendota Mental Health Institute, 301 Troy Drive, Madison, Wisconsin.

CHAPTER X

SUBSTITUTE CARE: FOSTER CARE

Foster care is substitute family care for a planned period of time when the child's own family cannot provide adequate care and adoption is neither desirable nor possible. Someone else takes over all aspects of the parental role temporarily.

Following supportive and supplementary services, foster care placement represents the third line of defense after every attempt has been made to maintain the child in the home. The placement involves an upheaval in the child's life; home environment, school, and peer associations are disrupted. The relationship with parents and siblings is likewise altered. There is a change in legal custody from the natural parents to the state. The state allocates the responsibility for the child's daily needs to the foster parents. Guardianship, which involves consent for surgery, marriage of a minor, and representation with the law remains with the natural parents.

Society's priority is toward strengthening the family to lessen the need for foster placement. If placement is necessary, it should be seen as a temporary measure until the family can be reunited. Underlying the foster care program is the assumption that the child using this service has had a difficult time with many unresolved conflicts and unmet needs. A simple change in environment with attention toward the meeting of basic physical needs is not enough. The foster home must attend to the child's total needs and development. The attempt to meet the child's total needs, including feelings of security and continuity in a program designed to be temporary, poses many problems. The goals of foster care are difficult to realize at best.

Types of Foster Homes

Foster care service delivery takes many different forms:

A. Boarding Homes
B. Receiving Homes
C. Free Homes
D. Specialized Foster Homes
E. Group Homes

Most foster homes are boarding homes. The agency finds and approves private homes for the temporary care of a specified number of children. The state pays a set rate per child in placement.

Receiving homes are maintained by the state to provide emergency placements. Receiving home placements must be brief. Every effort is made to move the children quickly into more appropriate facilities.

Free homes also exist. No payment is made for the child's care. The child may work to contribute to the family. In some cases, the family may plan to adopt the child.

Specialized foster homes have been developed for children with physical or emotional handicaps. The foster parents are often trained to meet these special needs. The financial compensation may be higher than that for regular foster placements.

Group homes represent a growing trend in foster care. They are agency operated and ideally suited for six to eight children. The group home, which is supervised by trained house parents, provides the personalization of a family with a less intense parent-child relationship. This setting provides the opportunity for developing peer relationships and has been most successful for adolescents whose developmental tasks make foster family placement difficult. Group homes have also been set up as halfway houses, aiding in the child's transition from the institution to the family.

Foster Parents

Foster parents primarily come from upper-lower or lower-middle class families. The mother may be interested in supplementing the family income. Although she has no specialized training, she has good home-making skills. She defines herself primarily by her maternal role. Home and family are highly valued.[1]

The number of foster homes is inadequate to meet the existing need. Active recruitment is necessary. Many agencies have central home finding departments.

[1]Kadushin, A., Child Welfare Services, New York, Macmillan Publishing Co., 1980, p. 330.

Mass media advertising is widely used. Experienced foster parents are effective recruiters of other families.

Foster parents have organized nationally. In Chicago in 1971, the First National Conference on Foster Parents was held. Conferences have been held annually since that time. The national organization has also developed a statement of beliefs, "The Rights of Foster Parents." These rights include the first option for adoption and the right to a hearing before returning a child to his biological parents. The philosophy that psychological parenthood takes precedence over blood ties and that continuity for the child takes precedence over the rights of the biological parents characterizes the thinking of the organization.

Social Work and Foster Care

Foster care is generally used when the situation is so severe that it is not easily corrected by supportive and supplementary services. In deciding to make a placement, the worker must examine a number of conditions. The danger to the child's present well-being and development is of primary concern. The capability and willingness of the parents to change is considered, as well as the availability of support systems to maintain the child in the home. The strengths and vulnerabilities of the child may help in determining whether remaining in the home situation or foster placement will be most traumatic and problematic. The child's coping capacity and ability to adapt to new situations should be considered.

If all attempts to maintain the child in the home fail and placement is deemed necessary, the agency attempts to match the child to an appropriate home. The social worker helps the child to separate from the biological family and become integrated into the new home. The worker maintains contact with the foster family to help with problems that arise and to ensure that the child receives proper care.

Once foster placement is made, the agency must balance its work among the natural parents, the child, and the foster parents.

Social Work Services for the Natural Parents

An attempt is made to keep the natural parents
involved throughout the entire placement. The natural
parents' involvement in the placement process through
letter writing and scheduled visitation can do much to
ease the adjustment and enhance the experience for the
child. The worker's primary concern is helping the
parents to make the necessary changes to enable the
child to return home. This is done through specific,
systematic case planning. A concrete goal-oriented
approach is useful. The worker must also deal with
the feelings of these parents. Feelings of anger, sad-
ness, guilt, and at times, relief, are common at the
time of placement. The more involvement the agency
maintains with the parents and the shorter the duration
of the placement, the more likely it is that the child
will be returned to the natural parents. In reality,
the heavy caseloads and time restraints often cause
the natural parents to be overlooked. Little help is
actually offered to these parents in many cases.

Social Work Services for Children

Children in placement have been called "orphans
of the living," being in emotional, social and legal
limbo.[2] The worker must help the child with separation from the biological home and the transition and
incorporation into the foster home. This is done by
helping the child to deal with personal feelings.
Feelings of rejection, guilt, anger, shame, fear of
abandonment, and fear of the unknown are all appropriate emotional responses of the child in placement.
The worker should provide the child with a clear and
honest explanation of the placement situation, connect-
ing the present life circumstances in foster care with
past experiences with natural parents. The worker
should help the child to deal with the problem of
divided loyalties. The child's feelings are most
accessible and workable early in the placement. The
worker will remain involved with the child as a stable
influence throughout the entire process. A clear
understanding of the placement and involvement with
the natural parents improves the chances for a good
adjustment by the child.

[2]Costin, Lela, Child Welfare: Policies and Practice,
New York, McGraw Hill, 1972, p. 328.

Social Work Services for Foster Parents

The agency must struggle with the question as to whether foster parents are clients or agency employees. The agency involvement with the foster parents includes the licensing of the home. Foster parents are also to be accountable to the agency which monitors the decisions involved in the child's care.

On the other hand, the social worker works with the foster parents to provide support and sanction in the handling of the child. The worker must help the foster parents accept the temporary nature of the arrangements. The worker helps the foster parents to accept the child and the natural parents. In addition, the worker is available to help the foster parents with all special problems as they arise.

The worker, in keeping to the overall case plan, must also plan for termination. This involves helping the child to prepare for another move and further emotional upheaval. If the child is to return to the natural parents, the child must be prepared for the adjustment problems involved in returning home. The foster parents must be supported in their efforts to help the child make a smooth transition back into the home.

Problems

Given the temporary nature of foster care, foster parents cannot become completely invested in the child. It is difficult to do any long-range planning for the child since the length of stay is often uncertain. There are an inadequate number of foster homes to fulfill all the needs for placement. Therefore, matching the child to the most suitable home is not always possible. The children who need placement are often difficult and demanding. The family may be unable to handle the child, resulting in moves to a series of homes with all the accompanying problems. The agency infringement on the privacy of the home and the inadequate payment of foster parents serve as deterrents in the recruiting of new foster parents.

Present Trends

Historically, children entering foster care remained there for long periods of time, often in a succession of homes. The emphasis now is on limited time placements and permanency. If the child cannot return home, efforts are made to terminate parental rights and find a permanent home for the child. Group homes are rapidly increasing in number and represent a growing trend in the area of child placement.

FOR STUDY AND DISCUSSION

1. Discuss the historical trends in foster care including the assumptions underlying our present attitudes.

2. The goal of providing for a child's needs for security and continuity in a temporary placement setting poses serious problems to those who are involved in foster care programs. Discuss the implications of this statement.

3. Devise a plan for the recruitment of foster homes. Be sure to build in methods to ensure quality control.

Student Exercises

These exercises are designed to complement the class presentation on foster care. In Exercise 1, students are asked to focus on positive childhood experiences which might be difficult to create in a foster care setting. Exercise 2 focuses on the difficult emotional issues which are involved in the process of foster care placement.

EXERCISE #1   TWENTY TREASURES

MATERIALS: Twenty Treasures Activity Sheet for each student

                     Pencils or pens

                     Newsprint and marker or blackboard and chalk

PROCEDURE:

1. The instructor begins by introducing the activity to the class:

> In today's lecture, we focused on some of the special challenges which are inherent to the foster care system, which attempts to provide physical and emotional nurturance in a temporary care program. The activity for this session will give you an opportunity to explore some of these specific problem areas from a more personalized perspective.

2. The instructor should give each student a copy of the Twenty Treasures Activity Sheet and continue with the following instructions:

> You've just received a copy of the Twenty Treasures Activity Sheet. In the left column, please make a list of twenty treasures or gifts which you received from your family during your childhood. These treasures may be specific (i.e. bicycle) or general (i.e. toys), tangible (i.e. clothing) or intangible (i.e. love). They may be treasured experiences or treasured role examples, treasured attitudes or treasured beliefs. Anything which you recall as a positive family

contribution to your life is appropriate.

NOTE: If there are any students in your class whose childhood experiences make it difficult to compile this list, suggest that they make a hypothetical treasure list of desirable gifts.

Allow five to ten minutes for this segment of the exercise. Encourage students to fill in as many items as possible. If students cannot complete their lists in ten minutes, continue the activity and encourage students to fill in the remainder of their lists after class.

3. Once students have completed their lists of treasures, ask them to code their lists in the columns on the right side of the activity sheet using the following symbols. List the symbols on a newsprint or blackboard for reference.

Column 1: Place a "+" next to those items which could easily be acquired in a foster home, a "-" next to those which would be difficult to acquire, a "?" next to any items which you are not sure about.

Column 2: Place a "T" next to the items which are tangible, an "I" next to those items which are intangible.

Column 3: Place a "$" next to those items which would be more expensive than the standard foster care allotment. Leave remaining items blank.

Column 4: Place a "*" next to the five items on your list which you value as your most treasured treasures. Leave remaining items blank.

Column 5: Place a "SW" next to the five items which you view as the most crucial adjustment items that the social worker should focus on. Leave remaining items blank.

4. Once students have completed the coding activity, ask them to fill in the sentence completions at the bottom of the activities sheet. Give the

following instructions:

> Based on your responses to the Twenty
> Treasures activity, please fill in the
> sentence completion section at the bottom
> of your sheet.

PROCESSING:

1. Move around the class asking students to share
   one of their sentence completion responses.
   These responses can provide the basis of class
   discussion.

2. Focus the group attention on Column 5 on the
   activity sheet. Ask group members to report on
   their choices. You may want to make a composite
   list of key focus areas.

TWENTY TREASURES ACTIVITY SHEET

Treasures	#1	#2	#3	#4	#5
1					
2					
3					
4					
5					
6					
7					
8					
9					
10					
11					
12					
13					
14					
15					
16					
17					
18					
19					
20					

I learned _____

I realized_____

I was surprised to find_____

I need to remember_____

EXERCISE #2   FOSTER CARE WISH LIST

MATERIALS: Foster Care Wish List Activity Sheet
for each student

Paper and pens or pencils

Newsprint and markers or
blackboard and chalk

PROCEDURE:

1.   The instructor begins by introducing the activity
to the students:

> Today's activity will focus on some of the
> more elusive interpersonal issues in foster
> care placement. Much of the literature sug-
> gests that many problems in foster care
> placement stem from inadequate preparation
> and poor communication. In this exercise,
> we will try to uncover some specific problem
> areas which might be overlooked by social
> workers in their efforts to provide prompt
> and efficient services to clients.

2.   Ask students to count off by threes to form
subgroups. Explain the appropriate roles to
class members:

> To help us uncover some of the unspoken needs
> and wishes which may be operating in a foster
> care placement setting, each of you will be
> asked to assume the role of the three client
> participants in a foster care placement.

> Group #1:   You will assume the role of the biolo-
> gical parent who is forced to place a
> child in foster care.

> Group #2:   You will assume the role of the foster
> parent who is bringing a new foster
> child into your family.

> Group #3:   You will assume the role of a foster
> child who is being placed in the foster
> care. Select any age range which
> interests you.

3. Distribute appropriate activity sheets to students in each group and explain the specific task:

> Please take a few minutes to reflect on the thoughts and feelings which you might experience if you found yourself in your designated role. There are some reactions which you would probably feel quite comfortable expressing. There are others which you might be more reluctant to voice. Focus on the latter area and write down two of the more personal wishes or messages which you might want to give to each of the other parties in the placement process. Your wishes or messages might reflect your personal fears or concerns at the time of placement or they might be requests for certain behaviors from others. Try to give messages which convey the more personal aspects of the experience which are difficult to express.

Allow five to ten minutes for students to write their messages.

PROCESSING:

1. Ask students to share their wishes or messages with other members of their subgroup. Allow five minutes of discussion.

2. Return small groups to full class discussion. On large sheets of newsprint or a blackboard, develop four composite lists of the unspoken wishes (i.e. messages to biological parents, messages to foster parents, messages to children, messages to social workers).

3. Drawing from the information on these lists, conduct a summary discussion. Your questions might include the following topics:

   a. What insights do you gain from these lists?

   b. Why are these wishes frequently unspoken?

   c. Whose unspoken messages are most frequently overlooked in a foster care placement? Why?

d.   What can the social worker do to encourage
     clients to share more of their personal
     needs and feelings?

e.   Do you think the social worker would also
     have unspoken messages which would not be
     given to clients?   What might these messages
     be?

FOSTER CARE WISH LIST

Role #1: <u>Biological Parent</u>

Wishes to Foster Parent

1.

2.

Wishes to Child

1.

2.

Wishes to Social Worker

1.

2.

FOSTER CARE WISH LIST

Role #2: <u>Foster Parent</u>

Wishes to Biological Parent

1.

2.

Wishes to Child

1.

2.

Wishes to Social Worker

1.

2.

FOSTER CARE WISH LIST

Role #3: <u>Child</u>

Wishes to Biological Parents

1.

2.

Wishes to Foster Parents

1.

2.

Wishes to Social Worker

1.

2.

References

"CWLA Statement on Foster Care Services," Child Welfare 58 (1), 1979, pp. 49-50.

Fanshel, D. & Shin, Children in Foster Care: A Longitudinal Investigation, New York, Columbia University Press, 1978.

Fanshel, D., "Preschoolers Entering Foster Care in NYC: The Need to Stress Plans for Permanency," Child Welfare 58 (2), 1979, pp. 67-81.

Galaway, B., "Path: An Agency Operated by Foster Parents," Child Welfare 57 (10), 1978, pp. 667-674.

Geiser, R., The Illusion of Caring, Boston, MA. Beacon Press, 1973.

Jenkins, S., Paths to Child Placement, New York, NY. Community Council of Greater New York, 1966.

Krymow, V.L., "Obstacles Encountered in Permanent Planning for Foster Children," Child Welfare 58 (2), 1979, pp. 97-104

McAdams, "The Parent in the Shadow," Journal of Public Social Service, Vol. 1 No. 4, 1970.

Magura, S., Claburn, W.,"Foster Care Case Review: A Critique of Concepts and Methods," Journal of Social Welfare 5 (2), 1978, pp. 25-34.

Shapiro, D., Agencies and Foster Children, New York, NY, Columbia University Press, 1976.

Steiner, G., The Children's Cause, Washington, D.C., The Brookings Institution, 1976.

Wiltse, K.T., "Foster Care in the 1970's: A Decade of Change," Children Today 8 (3), 1979, pp. 10-14.

Child Welfare League of America, Standards for Foster Family Services, New York, NY, 1975.

Audio Visual Materials

Jane, Audio Visual Services, The Pennsylvania State University, University Park, PA 16802.

<u>Kate</u>, Audio Visual Services, The Pennsylvania State University, University Park, PA 16802.

<u>Long View from a Dark Shadow</u>, Audio Visual Services, The Pennsylvania State University, University Park, PA 16802.

CHAPTER XI

SUBSTITUTE CARE: ADOPTION

Adoption is the change in legal guardianship of
the child. It allows individuals to become parents
through a legal and social process rather than a biological one. Adoption provides children for childless
couples and parents for children who are unable to
remain with their biological parents.

Adoption is a child-oriented practice with the
goal of providing fit parents for children with the
need for a permanent home and family. These services
are based on the underlying assumption that a child
needs the homelife, affection, security, and continuity that are available within a family. Once a child
is available for adoption, society has the responsibility to find a home for the child. In our society
today, it is not a private matter.

Adoptable children come from a variety of sources.
The largest source are those born to unwed mothers.
Children are also available for adoption when they are
abandoned, orphaned, or voluntarily surrendered by
their parents. An increasing number of foreign-born
children without families, or without families who can
care for them, are being adopted by American families.
Finally, in extreme cases, our legal system can permanently terminate the rights of parents who prove
themselves incapable of caring for their children.
The criteria for this legal action vary from state to
state.

Children of Unwed Mothers

The children of unwed mothers provide the major
source of children available for adoption. Although
the number of pregnancies among unmarried women continues to increase, the number of children available
for adoption has greatly decreased. This is due to
a number of changes in our society. With the changing
sex norms, there is more sexual activity among unmarried people, which increases the risk of pregnancy.
On the other hand, with the availability of improved
birth control methods and legal abortions, there is a
decrease in the number of children being born. Also,
increasing numbers of unwed mothers are keeping their
babies. The putative father is beginning to take a

more active role in the life of his child. In court decisions, he is increasingly gaining decision-making rights and responsibilities.

The Adoption Process

Requirements of the parents

Most couples are seeking to adopt a "desirable child." For most potential adoptive parents, a "desirable child" is a healthy, white infant. When a couple applies to become adoptive parents, they must meet the requirements set by the agency. Some of the guidelines for accepting adoptive parents for newborn babies are as follows:

> 35-45 years optimum age range
> Good physical and emotional health
> Financial stability
> Good marital relationship
> Acceptable motivation for adoption

Under some circumstances, the agency requires proof of infertility and an indication of an adequate adjustment to the condition. Some states require that the parents be of the same religion as the biological parent. In others, the biological parent has the right to decide the religion of the adoptive couple.

As the supply of "desirable children" decreases and the demand increases, the requirements become more stringent. Agencies report long waiting lists and many are refusing to take applications for newborn babies. Some agencies have completely closed their adoption departments. The remaining agencies are shifting their emphasis toward the placement of the hard-to-place children. The requirements for those willing to take hard-to-place children are much more lenient than the requirements for obtaining "desirable children." With an increase in age, health problem or handicap, the child becomes more difficult to place.

Role of the Social Worker

Society has the responsibility to protect the rights of the biological parents, the child, and the adoptive parents. With the goal of permanency and continuity, the assessment of the prospective parents and the child to ensure a successful placement is of great importance.

The social worker has the responsibility for working with the biological parents, adoptive parents, and the child. The worker has a supportive function throughout the process. The service to biological parents involves helping them to make a decision that they can live with. Once the decision is made, the worker helps them through the process and protects their right to anonymity. The role with the child is a protective one, ensuring that the adopted child has a good home. The worker helps the adoptive parents to bridge the gap between the expectations and realities of parenthood.

Once the placement is made, the adoptive family has a six-month to one-year trial period. During this time, the child remains under the guardianship of the agency. The trial period is for everyone's protection. If the family is not able to provide a good home for the child, the child can be removed at once. If the child develops an abnormality and the adoptive parents change their minds or if the parents change their minds about parenthood in general, the child can be removed and made available for another home. In protecting the adoptive parents this way, the law also protects the child from growing up unwanted in the home. In reality, removal from an adoptive home is rare, involving less than two percent of all placements. At the end of the trial period, the adoption is final. A new birth certificate with the adoptive parents' names is issued and the record is sealed to provide confidentiality for everyone.

Problems

The major problem facing the field of adoption is that there are fewer white healthy infants available for adoption than applicants desiring these children. This means that many couples wishing to adopt a child are unable to do so. The parents must pass a test of adequacy that natural parents are never confronted with. Once they are accepted, they must go through a long, drawn out process, never knowing if or when the child will arrive.

The agency involvement infringes on the couple's privacy. In our society, the concept of "natural parent" is valued as is evidenced by the use of the

terms "natural" versus "adoptive" parent. This emphasis makes it harder for the adoptive parent to feel
like a real parent.

Most adoptive placements are successful and there
is little evidence that an adopted child will have
significantly more emotional problems than children who
remain with their biological parents. The problem
areas do exist, however. The child may have a problem
with self-identity since knowledge about biological
background is lacking. The child may have difficulty
in developing a positive self-image, given the knowledge that the biological parents rejected their roles
as parents. Some children tend to idealize the unknown
natural parent. Especially at times of conflict with
the adoptive parents, the adopted child may be inclined
to polarize feelings, seeing one set of parents as good
and the other as bad.

Special Issues in Adoption

Telling

All adopted children should be told that they are
adopted. Ideally, the process is gradual, beginning
at a young age and continuing as the child's capacity
for understanding becomes more developed. Between the
ages of six and twelve, the child is able to develop
a realistic image of adoption. Around eight or nine,
the child's level of interest peaks. Success in telling
is based on the parents' comfort with the situation.
Overemphasis as well as avoidance are equally indicative of discomfort and can ultimately be problematic.
Emphasis in the telling should center on the fact that
the child was and is wanted and loved. Research indicates that children want to know, but wait for the
parents to initiate the discussion.

Search

Adoption represents the legal dissolution of the
relationship between the biological parent and the
adopted child. However, this legal agreement does not
guarantee the total termination of all contacts between
biological parents and members of adoptive families.
At some point in the life of an adopted child, it is
likely that the child will seek out the biological
parents or the biological parent(s) will search for the
child. While this search may prove to be disruptive,

it is also frequently quite valuable.

The Child Welfare League of America supports the premise of the sealed record and the pledge of confidentiality. The organization will tend to help an individual to obtain background information if requested, without providing identifying information. For good cause, as in a case when an adopted child needs genetic information, a court order can be obtained to open the records.

Independent Adoptions

Independent adoptions are those that take place without the use of an agency. Although many adoptions take place independently, the trend is increasingly toward using an agency. In independent adoptions there is no red tape to deal with, but there are no screenings, supports, or protections either. Independent adoption enables couples who were rejected by agencies to adopt a child. While agency adoption is child-oriented, independent adoptions are oriented toward the needs and desires of the adoptive couple. The only criteria for obtaining a child is the ability to pay.

Independent adoption may refer to a number of different procedures. The biological parents may make their own contact with someone they know or know of, who wants to adopt a child. Gray market adoptions involve doctors and lawyers who make all the arrangements for a fee. Black market adoptions are actual business transactions where a baby is sold for exorbitant fees. "Baby farms" have sprouted up in several places around the country where young girls are paid to become pregnant and give birth to adoptable children. Recruiters at the abortion clinics and the "baby farms" have been associated with the black market. These are currently under investigation.

Subsidized Adoptions

Subsidized adoption enables some children to be adopted who would otherwise be unadoptable, such as a handicapped child requiring expensive, special medical care. It also enables couples to adopt who would otherwise be unable to do so, such as foster parents with motivation and capability who lack in financial resources. Subsidized adoption grew out of the need to provide a permanent home for hard-to-place children. Subsidies may be in the form of a one-time grant or as ongoing payments. The regulations vary from case to case and from state to state.

International Adoption

There is an increasing interest in the United States in adopting children from other countries. This is due to a number of factors. There is a growing human concern for displaced children who are abandoned or orphaned as a result of a postwar upheaval. Following the Viet Nam War, there was an influx of Vietnamese children adopted here. There are more adoptive applicants than available American infants. With our increasing mobility and industrial expansion, many American couples are living abroad and making their contacts during their stay in another country.

The World Convention on Adoption Law has developed a uniform law throughout the world. The Travelers Aid International Social Service organizations, with branches in many countries, handle a large percentage of the international adoptions. They must first certify that the child is available for adoption, and then must take care of the complex paperwork to enable the child to be adopted in the United States.

The Child Welfare League of America feels that adoption outside the child's own country should be made only when plans cannot be made within the country of origin. Placement outside the familiar socio-cultural environment poses additional adjustment problems for the child. Adoption outside of the country inhibits the development of child welare services in that country. The league recommends that emphasis in the United States should be on placing the hard-to-place American children presently available for adoption.

Termination of Parents' Rights

When the parent is unwilling or unable to care for the child, the parental rights may be permanently terminated. In pursuit of permanency, all efforts are made to reunite the family quickly. When these efforts fail and the specified conditions remain unmet, parental rights may be terminated. This may be achieved by working with the biological parents to obtain their consent or through court action by the state protective

162

service agencies.

Changes in Adoption

The definition of adoptable is continually changing. Older, handicapped children, as well as sibling groups, are being adopted. Increasing numbers of transracial adoptions are occurring. Innovative recruitment methods are being employed to attract parents for these hard-to-place children. Publicity in the form of pictures and stories in the news media, as well as generalized advertising, has made it possible to find homes for many children with special needs. The distinction between foster parents and adoptive parents is narrowing. Adoptive parents are organizing and are increasingly involving themselves in matters related to adoption. The requirements for adoptive parents are also changing. Single parents (men and women), homosexual couples, and other untraditional family forms are being accepted as adoptive parents for hard-to-place children. An adoption resource exchange has been developed. This provides information on all available children to all agencies throughout the country in the interest of finding a permanent home for as many children as possible.

FOR STUDY AND DISCUSSION

1. The requirements for parents willing to take "hard-to-place" children are much more lenient than those for obtaining "desirable children." Discuss the implications of this statement.

2. Although many adoptions are handled independently, there is an increasing trend toward the use of an agency. Discuss the pros and cons to both agency and independent adoption.

3. Adoption has undergone many changes in the past two decades. Discuss some of these changes and the reasons behind them.

Student Exercises

These exercises serve two distinct purposes.
Exercise 1 focuses on the topic of adoption by presenting five potential dilemmas which could confront
the adoption social worker. Exercise 2 is designed
to help students to begin an informal process of future
career assessment in the field of child welfare.

EXERCISE #1: DILEMMAS FOR THE ADOPTION AGENCY

MATERIALS: One set of dilemma cards for each
subgroup

PROCEDURE:

1. The instructor begins by explaining the activity
to the class:

> Those child welfare workers who become in-
> volved in adoption work inevitably face many
> difficult situations. In their efforts to
> balance the needs and wishes of biological
> parents, adoptive parents, and children, social
> workers are often called upon to make extreme-
> ly difficult choices.

> Today, we're going to take a look at some
> hypothetical dilemmas which could confront
> the social worker in an adoption agency.
> You will each have an opportunity to offer
> your solutions to some of the more ambiguous
> conflicts which complicate the adoption
> process.

2. Divide the class into subgroups with no more than
five students per group. Continue with specific
instructions for the activity:

> Each group will receive a package of cards
> with hypothetical adoption related problems.
> To begin the exercise, one group member will
> select a card, read the problem aloud to the
> group, and respond to the situation, assuming
> the role of the adoption social worker. Once
> the first speaker has responded, other group
> members will have an opportunity to react to
> the first speaker's comments. This process
> will be repeated until each student has

164

selected one problem card. Time limitations make it necessary for us to move quite rapidly through each problem. Try not to get too frustrated!

3. Distribute packages with five problem cards to each group. Topics for these cards can be found at the end of this exercise. Instruct groups to begin. Allow approximately five minutes for each dilemma, three minutes for the initial speaker's response, and two minutes for group reaction. Repeat the process until every student has responded to at least one problem.

PROCESSING:

1. In a brief closing discussion with the full group, summarize the small group reactions to this exercise. You may want to raise some of the following topics for discussion:

    a. Which problem situations seemed most difficult? Why?

    b. Were there differences of opinion among group members? If so, what does this suggest to you about the realistic solution of these problems?

    c. When the personal opinion of the social worker and agency policy conflict, how should the worker go about resolving the conflict?

    d. What other problems can you think of which might arise in adoption cases?

    e. What have you learned from this activity?

ADOPTION DILEMMAS

1. An infant has been successfully placed with an adoptive family. After four months, everything seems to be going smoothly when the biological father comes to you and demands that the child be returned to him. He is unmarried and only working part-time. How would you respond?

2. You receive an adoption application from a homosexual couple who express an interest in adopting a handicapped child. How would you respond?

3. You have been working with a couple who are extremely eager to adopt. The couple meet all of the agency criteria and appear to be particularly well-suited for parenthood. However, a thorough check of the family history shows that the couple has failed to report one important piece of information. The wife had been involved in a teenage marriage, which lasted four months, fifteen years earlier. If this information were included in the couple's application, they would be rejected automatically from further consideration as adoptive parents. How would you respond?

4. You are working with an unmarried mother who wants to give up her infant for adoption. During your discussion, she mentions that a neighbor had recommended that she contact a baby black market source where they had "bought" their adopted son two years ago. How would you respond?

5. After two years of adoptive parenthood, a couple returns to your agency. Their adopted child has developed serious physical handicaps which cannot be corrected. The adoptive parents no longer wish to keep the child. How would you respond?

EXERCISE #2:   IS CHILD WELFARE FOR YOU?

MATERIALS: Child Welfare Self-Examination Sheets
               for each student

               Pens or pencils

               Newsprint and markers or
               blackboard and chalk

PROCEDURE:

1.   The instructor begins by explaining the activity
     the students:

          The time has come to think about moving from
          the theoretical realms of the classroom into
          the practical realms of real agencies with
          real clients and real problems. In this
          course, we've worked together to explore the
          current theories and practices in the field
          of child welfare. Now it's up to you to de-
          cide whether this area of social work is the
          one for you. To help you along in your
          decision making process, I'm going to ask
          each of you to complete an activity sheet
          which will allow you to explore some of the
          critical questions.

2.   Hand out an activity sheet to each student. Allow
     enough time for students to respond to each
     question.

PROCESSING:

1.   In a full group discussion, develop a composite
     list of the responses to Questions 1 and 2.

2.   Ask for volunteers who are willing to identify
     those areas where they might need more training
     and/or education. Whenever possible, encourage
     the group to identify potential resources which
     could be utilized to meet specific needs (i.e.
     written resources, course work, agency contacts,
     etc.).

3.   Conclude the exercise by asking students to share
     their individual responses to the last question on
     the sheets.

CHILD WELFARE SELF-EXAMINATION SHEET

DIRECTIONS: Drawing on your experience from this
                class and any relevant field work ex-
                periences, please answer the following
                questions.

1. What do you see as some of the advantages or
    attractions of working in the area of child
    welfare?

    _____

    _____

    _____

    _____

    _____

2. What do you see as the negative aspects of a job
    in child welfare?

    _____

    _____

    _____

    _____

    _____

3. If you were to pursue child welfare work, which
    area(s) would be most attractive to you?

    _____

    _____

    _____

    _____

    _____

    _____

4. What are some of your current strengths which would help to make you a good child welfare worker?

_____

_____

_____

_____

_____

5. What are some of your weaker areas which need development?

_____

_____

_____

_____

_____

6. If you decided to work in the child welfare area, in what areas would you want further education?

_____

_____

_____

_____

_____

7. What skill areas would you like to work on to become a better child welfare worker?

_____

_____

_____

8. What specific steps could you take to further your education and skills training?

_____

_____

_____

_____

_____

9. Who could you contact to give you some assistance?

_____

_____

_____

_____

_____

10. Based on your answers to the preceding questions, do you see child welfare work as an attractive career choice for you?

Yes _____   No _____

Why? _____

_____

_____

_____

_____

_____

References

Gallagher, V.M., "What's Happening in Adoption?" Children Today, 4 (6), 1975, pp. 11-13, 36.

Grow, L., Black Children - White Parents, A Study of Transracial Adoption, New York, NY, CWLA, 1974.

Jones, M.L., "Preparing School Age Children for Adoption," Child Welfare, LVIII, No. 1, January 1979, pp. 27-34.

Katz, L., "Adoption Counseling as a Preventive Mental Health Specialty," Child Welfare, LIX, No. 3, March 1980, pp. 161-167.

Katz, L., "Older Child Adoptive Placement," Child Welfare, March 1977.

Spencer, M.E., "The Terminology of Adoption," Child Welfare, LVIII, No. 7, July/August 1979, pp. 451-459.

Thompson, P., "Stresses in the Adoption Process: A Personal Account," Social Work, Vol. 23, May 1978.

Ward, M., "The Relationship Between Parents and Caseworker in Adoption," Social Casework, Vol. 60, No. 2, February 1979, pp. 96-103.

Child Welfare League of America Standards for Adoption Services, New York, NY, CWLA, 1978.

Audio Visual Materials

Chosen Child, Partslandz, Audio Visual Services, The Pennsylvania State University, University Park, PA, 16802.

I'll Never Get Her Back, Audio Visual Services, The Pennsylvania State University, University Park, PA, 16802.

Professor Greta Singer is a graduate of Queens College and received a Master's Degree from the Columbia University Graduate School of Social Work. After spending many years as a social worker, she joined the faculty of the Graduate School of Social Work at Rutgers University. For the past eight years she has been Professor of Social Work at Monmouth College where she coordinates the Social Work Program. Professor Singer has published many scholarly works in the field of Social Work. She has a private practice in individual and group therapy, specializing in marriage counseling.

Professor Marcia Rachlin is a graduate of the University of Pittsburgh and received a Master's Degree from the University of Pennsylvania School of Social Work. She has been employed as a social worker at Jersey Shore Community Mental Health Center and is currently a member of the Child Study Team at Rumson-Fair Haven Regional High School. She is also an Adjunct Professor of Social Work at Monmouth College specializing in Child Welfare.

Professor Maybeth Cassidy is a graduate of the University of Rhode Island and received a Master's Degree from the University of Rhode Island and Temple University. She has been involved in the fields of education and mental health for the past ten years. She is currently employed as Educational Director of the Monmouth County JINS Shelter. In addition, she provides private consulting services in teacher training and human services. She is also an Adjunct Professor of Education at Monmouth College.